Brighter Skies Ahead

Praise for Brighter Skies Ahead

"Deep in the frenzy of what Terri so eloquently calls the 'juggling act years', I had not taken much time to consider the seasons of life that come after this one. However, *Brighter Skies Ahead* isn't just for those who are already in their final seasons. It is full of advice, great ideas and inspiration for reflection for every stage of life. It's the blast of sunshine you would expect from Terri with an even more important 'winter life advisory' that I didn't even know I needed. It's been a blessing to have Terri as a mentor and now, thankfully, we all have access to her wisdom, wit and generosity."

—**Ginger Zee,** chief meteorologist at *ABC News*

"As parents, we often put our own dreams on the back-burner for a few decades so we can pour all of our energy into raising incredible kids. In *Brighter Skies Ahead*, DeBoer takes readers on an entertaining, uplifting, informative, and sometimes funny journey, encouraging them to 'Dream Big' as they empty the nest."

—**Bob Goff,** *New York Times* bestselling author of *Love Does, Everybody Always,* and *Dream Big*

"Providing a fresh, insightful, and honest look at the mixed emotions parents face when our young adults 'don't need us anymore,' DeBoer taps into the bittersweet moment we say goodbye, knowing life without them under our roof will never be quite the same, but also reminding us—and showing us—that our own futures are full of limitless possibilities. Engaging, relatable, and thoroughly entertaining."

—**Tracy Brogan,** *Wall Street Journal* and *USA Today* bestselling author and Amazon Publishing Diamond Award Winner for *Bell Harbor* and *Trillium Bay* series

"As a renowned meteorologist, Terri DeBoer knows how difficult it is to forecast each day of our weather. As a mother and empty nester, she also understands how hard it is to forecast life after your children grow up and leave home. *Brighter Skies Ahead* offers valuable lessons and deeply personal stories on how to navigate the seasons of our lives with hope, faith, wisdom, humor and inspiration. I predict it's going to be like a sunny day for countless readers."

—**Wade Rouse,** Internationally bestselling author of *The Clover Girls* (Pen Name: Viola Shipman)

"As a working mother raising three children, we were running faster than I can now even imagine we were capable of, and then they left on their own life journeys. Terri's stories in *Brighter Skies Ahead* are so timely and inspirational! Just what my husband and I need as we settle down into our next phase of life, rediscovering each other and our evolving role as parents."

—**Cathy Cooper,** Meijer senior director of community partnerships and giving/executive director, Meijer LPGA Classic

"Anyone in the midst of empty-nesting will benefit from Terri DeBoer's *Brighter Skies Ahead.* This phase is a natural part of life, so the inspiration and wisdom in this accessible and easy-to-read collection of essays will get you going on *you* again, especially in a world where there's so much change for men and women everywhere."

—**David Morris,** former publisher, Zondervan Publishing

"Although my Empty Nest season started fourteen years ago, it didn't stop me from reading *Brighter Skies Ahead* now. I recognized myself throughout the book and wish it had been available when I was experiencing those empty nest feelings. I plan on gifting *Brighter Skies Ahead* at graduations—not for the graduates but the parents who will be entering the Empty Nest season with us.

—**Tricia L. McDonald,** owner/operator Splattered Ink Press, author of *Life With Sally* series, *Quit Whining Start Writing*, and *The Sally Squad: Pals to the Rescue*

"I have been blessed over my career to have the privilege of caring for women through all seasons of life, including the emotionally painful season of emptying the nest. I prescribe *Brighter Skies Ahead* as an encouraging, uplifting, informative, and entertaining collection of essays that will help parents as they enter a new, and sometimes reluctant stage of their lives."

—**Dr. Renee Elderkin**, OB/GYN, attending physician, University of Michigan Health-Metro Campus, associate professor at Michigan State University, active member on the Board of Obstetrics/Gynecology, active member, American College of Obstetrics/Gynecology

"In her debut book, *Brighter Skies Ahead*, Terri DeBoer takes the highs and lows of empty nesting and articulates these in a way to offer hope, joy, and love for what can sometimes be painful but also exciting times of life. DeBoer's book is her journey but gives us the read like *My Big Fat Greek Wedding* did in a movie . . . "I have been there, I can relate, I have felt that way, I can laugh at myself." I suggest find a cozy winter day, a sunny summer day, or a crisp fall/spring day to enjoy this must-read book!

—**Christy Buck,** executive director, Mental Health Foundation of West Michigan

"As a mother of five, the passage to a quieter house happens faster than you think. Time to adjust to new roles and rediscover yourself. Terri's stories provide support and strategies in establishing a fulfilling next phase of life."

—**Peaches McCahill,** president of The McCahill Group

"I've already experienced one of my three children flying the coop. The other two are close behind. And while I work in the field of discovering a fulfilling encore stage of life, and can speak on it objectively, I hadn't found a resource to really help me personally navigate this stage in life until now. In *Brighter Skies Ahead,* Terri provides a light and thought-provoking guide that will help empty nesters (and those of us who are soon-to-be empty nesters) make this transition a little less daunting."

—**Jennifer Feuerstein,** associate state director, AARP Michigan

"We will each experience the process of emptying our nest in a different way and in our own time. In *Brighter Skies Ahead,* Terri takes us through many aspects of that change, helping to identify things that are most relevant for you in building a happy and productive next phase of life."

—**Julie A. Brinks,** vice president and general manager, WOOD-TV/WOTV/WXSP

"Terri has been forecasting her whole life, and in this new season as an empty nester and a grandpa, *Brighter Skies Ahead* is a must-read on my list for what lies ahead! We adapt to any weather; we can do the same for the Empty Nest season."

—**Rick Vuyst,** business owner, "Baby Bloomer," author, radio host at WOOD Radio

"I've worked with Terri professionally for decades and have always marveled at her positive attitude. Couple that attitude with her inquisitive nature as a scientist, and she made *Brighter Skies Ahead* a comprehensive and intuitive compilation of advice for what turned out to be a difficult period for my wife and me *spot on*. Thank you, Terri!"

—**Steve Kelly,** radio host for WOOD Radio Morning Show

Brighter Skies Ahead

Forecasting a Full Life
When You Empty the Nest

TERRI DeBOER

NASHVILLE

NEW YORK • LONDON • MELBOURNE • VANCOUVER

Brighter Skies Ahead
Forecasting a Full Life When You Empty the Nest

Published in New York, New York, by Morgan James Publishing. Morgan James is a trademark of Morgan James, LLC. www.MorganJamesPublishing.com

Morgan James BOGO™

A **FREE** ebook edition is available for you or a friend with the purchase of this print book.

CLEARLY SIGN YOUR NAME ABOVE

Instructions to claim your free ebook edition:
1. Visit MorganJamesBOGO.com
2. Sign your name CLEARLY in the space above
3. Complete the form and submit a photo of this entire page
4. You or your friend can download the ebook to your preferred device

ISBN 9781631955471 paperback
ISBN 9781631955488 ebook
Library of Congress Control Number: 2021935172

Cover and Interior Design by:
Chris Treccani
www.3dogcreative.net

Morgan James PUBLISHING Builds with... Habitat for Humanity® Peninsula and Greater Williamsburg

Morgan James is a proud partner of Habitat for Humanity Peninsula and Greater Williamsburg. Partners in building since 2006.

Get involved today! Visit
MorganJamesPublishing.com/giving-back

For my incredible family.
Thank you for filling my nest for so many years
and my heart forever.

Table Of Contents

Acknowledgments

Thank you so much to the original literary team who saw the value in the message, Tom Dean and David Morris.

Andy Rogers is an insightful editor who sculpted my words just as a potter would transform a lump of clay.

Tricia McDonald for using her life experience and publishing expertise to develop and perfect the message and manuscript.

David Hancock and the team at Morgan James Publishing for your partnership in bringing this book to readers. A special thank you to my Author Relations Manager Stephanie McLawhorn for professionally and patiently guiding me and this project through the publication process.

Cortney Donelson for sharing her editorial and technical expertise.

Tracy Brogan for countless hours of encouragement and support, and for using her creativity to come up with such an amazing TITLE for this book.

All of my colleagues (past and present), especially those at WOOD-TV for being such great teammates on my remarkable professional journey.

The hundreds of teachers, coaches, advisors, teammates, fellow parents, and friends who made an incredible impact on my life and the lives of my children

My Precious Family

My husband, Bill, for pushing me to pursue my dreams and making me believe in myself.

My children, Jacob, Jacqueline, Jennifer, Taylor, and Ben, for filling my life with hope, joy, laughter, and love. Watching all of you dream big and work hard has inspired me to reach for my own dreams.

My grandson Levi for showing me the joy in the simple things like playing in the sandbox and dunking "Grammy's head" underwater.

My parents, Ron and Helen Ferrucci, and my brother Ron, for a lifetime of unfailing love and support

My greatest gratitude is for the peace and hope through all seasons of life that comes from a relationship with Jesus Christ and the love of our amazing Heavenly Father. Praise God that I am never alone in this empty nest!

Introduction

Our life unfolds in a series of seasons.

Life begins in a season we'll call Growing Up. Like newly hatched robins in the springtime, in this season, we learn, mature, and prepare to launch into the world on our own; as adults. This part of life is a time of preparation. In nature, this season includes tilling the soil and planting seeds. In life, this season involves learning and training, gaining knowledge and expertise that will become the cornerstone of our vocational and professional careers.

The next season could be called Young Adult. It features the beginning of life as a young adult, filled with ambition, hopes, and dreams for the future. This is the summer of life. During this season, we are launching our careers, often getting married and starting a family. This part of life is a period of transition, going from a "me-focused" life perspective to shifting the focus to others, our spouses, and children.

The following season is one best described as a complete Juggling Act. Like autumn, this season is filled with change. So much to do every day for everyone else; never enough hours in the day to get everything done. You can spend all day working, and the yard still needs raking. In fact, as a full-time working mother for many years, my life seemed filled with chaos. This is the same for so many people trying to keep it all together during the years when their kids are growing up. Sometimes, the thought of being all alone and having time that is your own without other people relying on you can seem like a far-off fantasy. But, like all things in life, the reality is the Juggling Act is just one season of life. It is temporary.

During winter, the world seems to settle. Snow covers the ground, and the nights grow longer. Winter is often a time to shift your focus in preparation for what lies ahead. The next season of life is similar. We move from being constantly needed as a parent back to being more of a "solo player." As our children grow and leave home, our schedules often become our own again. Our space becomes our own. Our financial resources become our own. This is the Empty Nest season. Making this transition has been the toughest stage of all.

Why is that? Why isn't the Empty Nest season easier to transition into? I've come to this realization, and maybe you feel this too: I often yearn to return to those chaotic years when I felt most needed!

As I began my struggle with emptying the nest, I reached out to others I know for advice, guidance, and comfort. After hearing the same emotions coming from people I turned to, I discovered that what I was feeling was not unique. In fact, learning of such widespread and common feelings of emptiness created a desire to help others experiencing this same painful life transition.

The purpose of this book is to help outline and identify this transitional period. It is intended as an easy-to-read guidebook filled with thoughtful and encouraging suggestions.

This book is not designed to be a deep dive into my life, nor is it a suggestion that my life as a parent was perfect. I am not a psychologist, counselor, or medical professional. I am a mother of three who tried my best as I dedicated three decades of my life to raising these incredible human beings. Did I make a few mistakes along the way? Of course, I did. We are all humans, so our relationships are not always perfect, even those close family relationships.

I hope this book will help you look forward to the next season in life, with the freedom and flexibility in time and resources to set new goals and chase new dreams.

LETTER TO ME

A few years ago, country music star Brad Paisley recorded a song titled, "Letter to Me." It's a poignant song that takes the singer on a journey back to the time he turned seventeen.

In the song, Paisley recalls formative experiences that seemed like incredible obstacles, like the time he ran out of gas while on a date with a girl he liked or when he got a ticket for running a stop sign. This song also talked about a special aunt who died much too soon. It includes other regrets, like wishing he would have taken Spanish or a typing class. The song also foretells the future family of the woman who would become his wife and mother of his children he didn't even MEET until several years after he graduated from high school.

The song became an anthem, with people all over the world using it as an inspiration to write their own "Letter" to their younger selves… a musical journey revealing the brevity of life, and the hope and promise that comes as the future unfolds.

If I could take a bit of poetic license with that concept, I would write a letter to myself the day I turned twenty-six. It was the single worst birthday I ever experienced, finishing the day all alone in my one-bedroom apartment in the bathtub with a bottle of champagne. Even though I was enjoying professional success, working as a television reporter, I was sad and lonely. I had just called off a wedding (my second failed engagement) and felt deep despair! I felt like a loser celebrating this birthday ALL ALONE! This birthday marked the march toward The Big 3-0, and I was experiencing what psychologists refer to as unrealized expectations for my life.

Little did I know the life that was waiting for me!

I could never have imagined that within a few short years, I would meet and marry the man of my dreams, complete a second college degree, and become a mother! I didn't know I would be hired away by my competitor to shift to a career path that would turn me into one of the most recognized and respected television personalities in West Michigan! My kids earned academic and athletic success at school, with busy schedules of practices, activities, rehearsals, games, and competitions.

So many days felt like life in the middle of a whirlwind, a hectic and incredible journey.

Now, that is all ending.

As I enter this new season of life, I am moving through another time of extreme challenge. I have two married children, a grandson, and my youngest child has just graduated from college. I am experiencing the emptiness of the empty nest. Instead of a bottle of champagne in the bathtub, I have found myself on the couch in my pajamas in the middle of the afternoon. Many of those emotions I felt in my mid-twenties are surfacing again.

This time, though, the despair is accompanied by grief, as I longingly look back at all those busy and wonderful years packed full of activities and adventures. The chaos of the unending lists of tasks seemed exhausting at the time but looking back now seems like a time of Utopia.

As often as I feel alone, I also realize I have tons of company in this new season. This Empty Nest season has been referred to in terms of a mid-life crisis or midlife malaise.

As I reflect on that twenty-six-year-old in the bathtub, I realize this, too, is just a temporary state.

Life is about moving forward.

For that woman in her mid-twenties, moving forward involved going back to college, getting married, and starting a family. In this Empty Nest season, my new path includes writing this book, starting a podcast, exploring new hobbies, and deepening my faith.

This book is written to share with you fifty short essays designed to offer hope, encouragement, comfort, and a few laughs as you join me in the journey toward breaking out of that "mid-life" state and moving toward your next adventure.

I hope this book provides you comfort, encouragement, and motivation, so you will join me by getting off that couch and taking action.

The Grass Is Greener In The Rearview Mirror

Life is divided into three terms
-that which was, which is and which will be.
Let us learn from the past to profit by the present,
and from the present, to live better in the future.
William Wordsworth

Chapter 1
Seasons of Life

—●—

sea·son (sē′zən) [1]
noun

1. one of the four natural divisions of the year, spring, summer, fall, and winter, in the North and South Temperate zones. Each season, beginning astronomically at an equinox or solstice is characterized by specific meteorological or climatic conditions.
2. a recurrent period characterized by certain occurrences, occupations, festivities, or crops: the holiday season; tomato season.
3. a suitable, natural, or convenient time: a season for merriment.
4. a period of time: gone for a season.

Ecclesiastes 3:1–8[2]

"For everything, there is a season, and a time for every purpose under heaven: a time to be born, and a time to die; a time to plant, and a time to pluck up that which is planted; a time to kill, and a time to heal; a time to break down, and a time to build up; a time to weep, and a time to laugh; a time to mourn, and a time to dance; a time to cast away stones, and a time to gather stones together; a time to embrace, and a time to refrain from embracing; a time to seek, and a time to lose; a time to keep, and a time to cast away; a time to rend, and a time to sew; a time to keep silence, and a time to speak; a time to love, and a time to hate; a time for war, and a time for peace."

As a meteorologist, I've spent my adult life (the past few decades) obsessed with seasons. More than thirty years translates into 120+ seasons. My professional life requires forecasting the always-changing weather; in West Michigan, a part of the country that features all four seasons.

As a *television* meteorologist, I've spent that same amount of time navigating through the tumultuous seasons of broadcasting and the media. When I started my broadcast television career, there were no cell phones, no websites, no social media, no Netflix® or Google® or Amazon® or Hulu®! In today's media world, the explosion of technology has created so many sources for people to find information and entertainment; it's a challenge to keep viewers connected to local television. Through all these changes, I've been fortunate to become an enduring constant in my local television market, even as the broadcast news industry has changed as dramatically and as frequently as the changing seasons and corresponding weather I've been forecasting. As with any successful career, I didn't do it alone. God has blessed me with supportive friends, inspirational mentors, and hard-working colleagues who have created an environment for stability and longevity. I will share stories from these relationships in the pages of this book.

As a working wife and mother (and now grandmother), my family has gone through the biggest series of changes over these decades. From walking down the aisle and saying "I Do" to becoming a mother to three active children with demanding schedules, who I proudly say have now reached adulthood as incredible human beings. I spent at least twenty-five of the past years in the middle of a "whirlwind." As a professional family woman, I've experienced those decades through different changing seasons.

Just as the weather and atmosphere are measured by seasons, so is life. The season of spring marks the beginning point as we are growing up and beginning our journey. Spring is a time of hope and transition. Just as spring storms mark the weather of the season, the transition into this season in life can have the strongest storms. Summer is the time when we are sailing along; starting and raising our families; progressing in our careers, balancing demands that go along with the rapid growth and change in so many different areas. Summer is often a time of so much activity; the days are the longest, and it's a good thing because there is more to do than there seems to be hours in a day. Fall represents that time of harvest when we reap the benefits of our hard work and investment in so many different areas. At work, we have achieved our career goals. At home, our children are graduating and going to college, getting married, and starting families of their own.

As we transition from late fall into winter, we are becoming empty nesters and retiring from that career or job we have loved. This is a time when people often become preoccupied with looking back and reflecting on all those seasons that have come before, wistfully wishing we could almost have a do-over of those times we remember with fondness and melancholy. Winter days are short, dark, and cold. Sometimes we find it hard to believe there were ever birds, flowers, or green grass on a frozen and desolate landscape.

But before you kick back and settle into a long, nostalgic look backward, let me share something with you I've learned from my years in meteorology.

There is a difference between weather and climate. Weather is a snapshot is a snapshot of current conditions, including temperature, humidity, wind, precipitation, cloudiness for a short period for a particular place. Weather is the overview for a few hours or perhaps a couple days. Depending on the season, some days are hot; some are cold; some are wet; some are snowy, and some are even pleasant.

Weather can be marked by storms and extremes.

On the other hand, climate represents a combination of all those weather conditions over several decades! So, even though parts of Florida may experience the occasional freeze, which may temporarily threaten the citrus crops, an average of the temperatures that occur over multiple decades reveals those freezing temperatures happen rarely. To be specific, the climate statistical model used by the National Weather Service, which is recognized to be the authority on climate information, takes a thirty-year average weather at a particular location for a specific date. This approach allows the variability from recent years to cold years and spikes of precipitation generated by storms and other extreme years to balance out over three decades. Since the weather is cyclical, driven by ocean currents and solar cycles, a thirty-year average gives a reliable number. From one day to the next, as the yearly climate calendar progresses, there is minimal change.

For example, in my local area of West Michigan, there may only be a degree or two change every day or two, depending on the time of year.

Knowing the climate data of a certain location will give the people who live there or visit a reasonable expectation of what conditions they will face in an average year.

Life circumstances could also be described in terms of weather and climate. Day-to-day activities and tasks are like the weather in our lives. Many days are quiet, with occasional showers and storms thrown in along with how we need to face or manage. Just as the climate in nature represents the thirty-year average of daily weather occurrences, our life's climate is the overall status of our lives. The climate of our lives includes our home, lifestyle, family and relationship status, and profession.

The year 2020 was marked by an unpredictable storm; the Coronovirus Pandemic. This killer virus kept many people on complete lock-down for months, as it proved to be easy to spread and deadly for certain members of society. Even as many of those lockdowns ended, a new reality emerged with people wearing face masks while in public and practicing a new concept called social distancing, where people were encouraged to stay at least six feet away from others during any sort of interaction.

Just like with the weather, we can try to prepare for these storms, but there is always a certain aspect of unpredictability. Powerful storms (like the Coronavirus Pandemic or Hurricane Katrina) will alter reality after they pass. Our best strategy is to prepare for as many of life's storms as possible, trusting our preparation will help us navigate even the unpredictable storms that swoop down upon us.

If we are not careful, as empty nesters, we can squander these years in life since we don't have as many frequent benchmarks or looming milestones. There can be a great temptation to live just waiting for the next storm to hit. From one day to the next, we may have some changes and challenges that demand our attention or disrupt the flow, but mostly one day will flow into the next and the next, like living through the weather or seasons' small changes from day to day. As we move through summer, for example, we may not notice the sun setting a minute or two earlier each day. But, by mid-late fall, there's no mistaking the fact it's dark by 6 p.m., when that used to be the time our golf league would tee off in mid-summer!

In order to take advantage of these years of our lives, we need to create our own new goals and permit ourselves to chase new dreams. This is a great time to search our soul for our passion, either trying something brand new or circling back to something we had put on hold for a few decades. You may have heard the phrase bucket list, where people write all the things they want to do before they kick the bucket. This list often includes important goals, like skydiving or traveling through Europe or Hawaii. While those big items are great aspirations, smaller activities that can be incorporated into a routine will provide a daily or weekly boost. Think about picking up the guitar again, working on your golf game, taking a class at the local community college (or even finishing that degree), becoming a volunteer for an organization that could use your passion and expertise, joining a bowling league or even starting a business.

Don't think of this as a selfish act. You are re-prioritizing your time, talent, and energy. After guiding the inhabitants in your nest to become their best selves, it's time to allow yourself the same opportunity.

LIVING A FULL LIFE

- Take out a notebook and write a list of the things in life you would like to achieve in the Empty Nest season. Dream Big!
- Prioritize that list.
- Write a step-by-step set of actions you need to take to accomplish the things on your list. If you don't know every step you need to take for a certain goal, try to write the first five steps you need to take toward that goal.

Chapter 2
What's Happening Now
What's Happening Next

———•———

What's happening now is what happened before,
and often what's going to happen again sometime or other.
Orson Welles

When we are in the Young Adult season, we are in the beginning stages of our journey into adulthood. We may take college classes, start a job, or even embark on the beginning stages of our career during this period in our lives.

For many of us, this is a time of self-discovery and self-improvement. It is also the time when we are self-centered, self-absorbed, and hopefully self-reliant. The WHY of this time is because this is our ALONE SEASON, also known as the Season of Self or the Season of Me. The life we have before us is, for the most part, a nearly empty canvas. We have the opportunity to try new things. If we decide we are on the wrong path or want to change the direction we are heading, we can often do so with minimal impact on the lives of anyone else.

This was why my life journey through my early twenties was relatively easy to navigate. I was bored with accounting, so I dropped out of college. While on that educational hiatus, I jumped from job to job, making new connections with people who would ultimately point me in a new direction. After finally graduating with a degree in television news broadcasting and working a couple of years, I pursued a specialized course of study in meteorology. When I made that decision, I devoted extra time, energy, and money to get advanced knowledge and training. I didn't have to support anyone else, nor did I have to get approval from anyone to follow this new dream. Since I was working in a television market that was much bigger than a beginning market, I expected to have to move to a much smaller city to transition from news reporter to an on-camera meteorologist. Since I was independent and un-attached, I was not in the least worried about taking that next step in my career upon the completion of my certification in Broadcast Meteorology.

Of course, I did not know I would fall in love with and marry a single dad just a few months into my program. I should say I fell in love with the total package of this sweet little boy and his dad. Because our love story included a child, we decided to get married fairly quickly. So, less than one year after meeting these two special men, we became an official family!

Suddenly, the answer to the question for me of "What's coming next?" had dramatically changed. I was no longer in the Season of Me. I had made the transition into the Season of We. I was no longer alone or independent; I was married with a child. Biology worked quickly for us, and less than two months after our wedding day, I was expecting another child. I was now a full-time working wife and mother, devoting my spare time to a course of study that seemed like a waste of time, energy, and money. Finishing my meteorology training no longer meant I would be guaranteed the opportunity to make the change from news to weather on air. Still, my husband and I decided I would follow through and complete the program.

PERSISTENCE

While earning my certification in meteorology, I learned an essential term for forecasting the weather, persistence. It says if you predict today's weather will be repeated tomorrow, you will, on average, be correct a majority of the time. This is considered one of the most accurate forecasting techniques for short-term weather in the business. So, when a meteorologist embraces the term persistence, they are indicating the current weather conditions are likely to continue. Overall seasons during a given year are often categorized as featuring an unusually high number of stretches of sunny and dry days or cloudy and cool days points to the reliability of the persistence model of forecasting.

When we apply the word persistence to our lives, it means a firm continuance in a course or action despite difficulty or adversity. As a new wife and mother, persistence for me often meant the daily cycle of work, studying, cooking, cleaning, shopping, playing and nurturing my new family. Perhaps you can look back on those days in your life and draw the comparison to the famous Bill Murray movie, *Groundhog Day*, in which life became a series of days that often felt like the same day repeated over and over and over again.

THE ONLY CONSTANT IS CHANGE

Of course, we know even the most persistent weather pattern (or series of life circumstances) eventually breaks down. Just like the weather changes, so too does life. Preparing for and forecasting changes in life involves a similar set of steps as forecasting the weather.

LOOK FOR CLUES

Before digging into the atmospheric conditions for specific time frames in the future, the most essential starting point is the current situation. Not only is it important to look outside at WHAT'S happening, it's also imperative to figure out WHY the weather is behaving the way it is at present. For example, if it's raining, what is causing the rain? Is it being caused by a warm front coming in or generated by a lake breeze convergence? Is it a pop-up instability shower or the beginning of a more intense line of storms approaching? In weather forecasting, understanding the WHY of the now is an integral part of correctly figuring out the WHAT of the next!

Meteorologists describe the atmosphere as a *system in motion*. That means there is always a "What's coming next?" to track. The same can be said of our lives, including being an empty nester. As we consider the journey of our lives, those are the exact two questions we need always to be asking ourselves:

- What's happening now?
- What's coming next?

THE WINDS OF CHANGE

The expansion of local news broadcasts to non-traditional times brought change to the television news industry. At my television station WWMT-TV in West Michigan, this meant the addition of a weekend morning newscast. Since I was nearing the end of meteorology training, I was given a chance to transition to on-air weathercaster for these newly starting newscasts.

The completion of my Broadcast Meteorology certification came with a husband, two children under the age of three, and a new position as Broadcast Meteorologist in a Top-40 television market.

 ## LIVING A FULL LIFE

- Which areas of your life challenge you to have persistence?
- Think about "What's happening now?" Why are these things happening?
- When you try to figure out "What's happening next?" what actions will you have to take?

Chapter 3
Timehop

The reason we struggle with insecurity is because we compare our behind-the-scenes with everyone else's highlight reel.

Steven Furtick

One of my favorite social media apps is Timehop. It's like a virtual trip down memory lane. It's available every day, grabbing all the pictures and social media posts for that date. Just like that . . . at your fingertips . . . you get the chance to see all the activities taking place on that date one, two, five, seven years ago. It's one of the first things I check every morning when I look through my social media, obsessively sometimes.

I try to figure out what I find most compelling about Timehop.

Is it because the memories that happened several years ago almost seem like they happened yesterday? Is it because we miss the past so much and think those were the good old days? Is it because the daily images are a collection of the highlights of the past several years that are available?

When you think about it, the only activities that ever make the cut on any social media are those that, by definition, are memorable. The highlights.

THE HOME RUN

It's like watching a sporting event on television. Even though most take a couple hours to complete, there are just a few big moments that will ever make up a highlight reel from that game. A baseball game where it is scoreless for several innings, and then there is a home run, which may win the game with a score of 1–0. Indeed, the very hitter responsible for that home run was likely up to bat several times that game. Each of those at-bats may not have been memorable. The batter could have struck out, walked, perhaps even made it on base. At the end of the day, each of those trips was not a part of the overall highlight reel of that game.

In fact, when you see the highlights on the eleven o'clock news, you don't see two hours, you only see about fifteen to thirty seconds. And of course, most of that time is spent replaying the big moment.

THE BEST STUFF

When we look at the collection of memories the Timehop app pulls together for us every day, we are only reliving the absolute best times.

While those images give us a warm and fuzzy feeling, mixed in with a bit of nostalgia, I believe there is significant danger in getting too caught up in the past. Those memories, while memorable, are also hand-picked and sanitized.

We see the pictures of our son or daughter posing with their AAU teammates with a trophy from a tournament and yearn for those special times. We may even forward some of those images to parents of former teammates, along with the phrase, "I miss those days."

But the Timehop of our lives in the Juggling Act season won't include the nights of two-hours of sleep. It won't show us getting home late, shuttling kids to practices or events, helping with homework or a special project, then making lunches for the next day. It won't show us washing uniforms, sewing costumes, folding clothes, loading, and then unloading the dishwasher, and finishing our work-related project or volunteer activity. Our highlight reels won't include the last-minute trips to the grocery store to get a healthy snack for the team or the hours spent preparing, serving, and cleaning up the team dinners. Nor will it show images from counseling and consoling a sobbing teenager through the pain of first heartbreak.

So, when we look back on our memories' sanitized versions, it is easy to remember only the good times. When those glory days seem too glorious, try checking out the social media feed of a young mom you may know who is still knee-deep in the Juggling Act season. I work with young people living in the Juggling Act season, like I did, as household names and recognizable faces in West Michigan; Teresa Weakley, Casey Jones, Matt Kirkwood, Emily Linnert, Jordan Carson, and Rachael Ruiz. Watching these incredible parents and professionals is like taking a walk down my memory lane. They have kids at home and the alarm clock screams at 2:30 a.m., or their work schedule extends into dinnertime. They are traveling the same road I did, having to look good, fresh (and rested) in front of a television camera. In some ways, the Juggling Act season might be like giving birth, in that I have mostly forgotten the pain and exhaustion of that season they are now living. I admire them for being involved parents, even though it means sacrificing rest. I should tell them more often what a great job I think they are doing. I often bite my tongue when I want to tell them I'm envious of the demanding and chaotic season of life they are living right now; and how I would trade places with them just to have my schedule packed with kids' activities and pressures, while dragging myself in front of the tv camera with only a few hours of sleep. I should also remind them how fast this season will come to an end and how they will miss the chaos. Even if you don't personally know someone who fits that description, a quick trip to the grocery store might put you face-to-face with a young parent who is not in a circumstance that will end up on a highlight reel.

There is one more danger in getting caught up in the past—missing out on the present's beauty and opportunity. In the future, we will likely look back on what's happening today and think longingly at this being one of the good old days.

 ## LIVING A FULL LIFE

- When you think about the good old days, are you realistic, or do you have a Timehop app on your memories, showing you only the highlights?
- Reflect on a typical day in the height of your busy Juggling Act season. Recall the emotions you were feeling. Was gratitude more prominent than stress and burn-out?
- Think about the people you know living through the Juggling Act season. Is there a way you could provide help to them by offering assistance, a word of encouragement, or some type of support?

Chapter 4
The Days Are Long.
The Years Are Short

———•———

When you worry and hurry through your day,
it is like an unopened gift thrown away.
Life is not a race. Do take it slower.
Hear the music, Before the song is over.
Timothy Ferriss, *The 4-Hour Workweek*

The household dynamic changed dramatically as each of my children graduated from high school and moved away to college. Since only two grades separated our oldest two children, Jacob's moving away to college left our family life still centered on the busyness of Jacqueline's high school activities and outside golf tournaments. At the same time, our youngest had middle school activities and travel sports as well. The transition was more difficult when Jacqueline moved away to college since it left the household more like that of an only child. Life remained busy, but with only one child at home,

21

sometimes the house was quiet. When Jenn was out on a weekend night or busy into the evenings; those occasions were introductions to the Empty Nest season lurking in our near future.

When my youngest daughter Jenn graduated from high school, it was difficult to close the door on that part of my life. My kids had been so active while they were growing up, especially during the high school years. With each of them playing multiple sports, the schedule every single season was jam-packed!

A successful journey through high school sports these days means almost year-round training and competition. So, not only is it just a series of activities going on during the actual season, the high-school athlete who is serious will dedicate significant effort into off-season skill development, workouts and contests.

That skill development and training starts as young as early elementary grades for athletes who want to reach their highest potential.

All three of my children took their sport into college, which meant they were serious. Of course, that meant our entire family was 100 percent committed to doing whatever it took for each to develop in that sport.

Even though my oldest two chose golf as their collegiate sport, they also played hockey, baseball, and softball. Hockey and golf are challenging sports for parents because of the extensive travel commitment. At one point, my daughter Jacqueline was on a travel hockey team that had a practice time that *ended* at 11:30 p.m. She was only in middle school so she would take a shower, put on her pajamas at the ice rink, and then climb into bed right when she got home. Even though my husband would typically be the late-night carpool driver, I could not fall asleep until they got home. As a morning news meteorologist, I was always on the super-early morning shift, with my alarm-clock ringing at 2:30 a.m. I never had much sleep on those practice nights.

Divide and conquer was typically the family plan. My husband and I would look at the schedule to figure out which child (or children) each of us would shepherd to practice or training.

We were full of adrenaline and short on downtime. It was a life on the go, and I loved it! I enjoyed having my time planned out for me.

During the Empty Nest season, all this busyness and the emotional energy that came with it, ends. The buzzer sounds. The game is over.

I took stock of the feelings of apprehension that flooded me at the time and came to an important realization about my personality. I'm a very task-oriented person. I enjoy having lots to do. In this world, there are people you could describe as thinkers and people who can best be described as do-ers. I fall into the latter category. I dislike downtime.

As my youngest child wrapped up her high school career, this do-er part of my life was ending as well. Not only was my family not going to be over-scheduled, I worried I would not be busy enough. My feelings were as much about me as they were about my children.

The key in making this transition was to think about how often I had put my life on hold while my kids were growing up. I needed to consider all those invitations declined throughout the year. As a local news media personality, I would receive invitations to attend special events like concerts, theater performances, or parties. When my kids were growing up, I would never want to commit to something special I wanted to do because I was too concerned something would come up on their schedule. I don't like to disappoint people, so I would politely decline an invitation, even if it was something I would want to do, just to absolutely positively make sure my schedule would be open if something came up with one of the kids.

At an end of the season party for my daughter's high school basketball team her senior year, I heard a parent make a statement I consider profound, "We are going from a year of lasts . . . to a year of firsts."

The last home game. The last road trip. The last team picture. The first day at a new school. The first practice with a new team. The first selfie with new friends.

"From a year of lasts, to a year of firsts." I kept that phrase close to my heart over the past years, as I looked back at those most special memories. Fortunately, it has become easier to think of that phrase when I'm experiencing something new or a recently discovered freedom, like enjoying an event I would have declined.

Indeed, the end of one season in our lives is the beginning of another. While those transitional periods are the toughest to navigate, the next season always comes with its own promise.

 ## LIVING A FULL LIFE

- Are you worried adjusting to the empty nest will leave you too many free hours?
- Are there invitations you pass on because you want to leave your schedule open for your kids?
- After a year of lasts, in what ways do you find yourself anticipating and/or dreading a year of firsts?

Chapter 5
What To Expect When You Are Expecting To Empty The Nest

———•———

Instead of wishing away nine months of pregnancy and complaining about the shadow over my feet, I'd have cherished every minute of it and realized that the wonderment growing inside me was to be my only chance in life to assist God in a miracle.

Erma Bombeck

When you find you're pregnant for the first time, *What to Expect When You're Expecting* is considered a must-read for every expectant mother. It is a week-by-week pregnancy guide written in 1984. The book is a perennial top-selling book on the *New York Times* bestseller list, almost considered a "-pregnancy bible.

This book covers *everything*, from morning sickness, fatigue, and stretch marks to moodiness, breast tenderness, and frequent urination. It's packed with all the information a pregnant woman would want to ask her sister, mother, best friend, or doctor.

The author of the book, Heidi Murkoff, created this masterpiece as she was searching for information during her first pregnancy! Her partners in this collaboration? Her mother (a freelance journalist) and her sister, (a nurse).

The book was so successful Murkoff created an entire collection of books aimed at walking mothers through pregnancy and into parenthood.

Week-by-week and month-by-month guides entitled:

- What to Expect the First Year
- What to Expect the Second Year
- What to Expect for the Toddler Years
- What to Expect/Eating Well when You are Expecting

There are pregnancy journals and an entire line of children's books under the same *Expecting* brand.

Almost no stone has been left unturned when it comes to topics a parent needs to know about parenting.

Of course, the one book missing from the lineup is *What to Expect When You're Expecting to Empty the Nest.*

It would have been nice to have a week-by-week guide through the transitional period of having no children left at home. So, here's my guide for you, designed to help frame the normal aspects that are a part of this monumental life change and give a "light at the end of the tunnel" for the coming weeks and months.

FIRST MONTH
Weeks 1–2:

Feelings: Sadness, separation anxiety, grief

Behaviors: Sudden crying; staring at family pictures for hours; lying in your child's bed; going to your child's closet, closing your eyes, and smelling left-behind clothing to get that familiar scent.

Weeks 3–4:
Feelings: Still sadness, also loneliness, boredom
Behaviors: Changing into pjs during the day; lying on the couch watching Hallmark® movies; drinking your favorite wine in the middle of the day, or eating a pint of ice cream.

SECOND MONTH
Weeks 1–2:
Feelings: Not as sad; missing the daily connection with child
Behaviors: Try to entice daily texting or phone calls with child; plan to meet for dinner.

Weeks 3–4:
Feelings: Not as sad; boredom and loneliness take over feelings
Behaviors: Discover YouTube®! (and enjoy daily video marathons).

THIRD AND FOURTH MONTHS
You realize the holiday season is just around the corner! Get energized to start house-cleaning, organization, and decoration.

Feelings: Excitement; energy; anticipation
Behaviors: Plan Thanksgiving menu; enjoy Christmas Shopping and wrapping the presents; tree decorating; plan menus; buy new games; stock up on everyone's favorite snacks and food.

FIFTH MONTH
*See also FIRST MONTH

Week 1:
Feelings: Sadness; grief; separation anxiety returns for the second time
Behaviors: Crying; hours spent looking at holiday pictures; sitting on child's bed.

Week 2:
Feelings: Boredom; Loneliness
Behaviors: Call friends to arrange activities: happy hours, movies, and shopping.

Weeks 3–4:
Feelings: A bit more energetic
Behaviors: Commit to a regular exercise routine.

SIXTH THROUGH NINTH MONTH
Adjusting to fewer commitments and a less rigid schedule

Feelings: Freedom; flexibility
Behaviors: Accept invitations to attend events; schedule appointments.

TENTH THROUGH TWELFTH MONTH
Finishing the final months of the first year as an empty nester.

Feelings: Proud of adjusting to a new normal; anticipation for the future
Behaviors: Setting long-term goals; plan a vacation; take a class; finish a degree.

GIVING BIRTH TO A NEW LIFE

From the moment the "+" shows up on a pregnancy test, new moms have many months to count down the arrival of the new member of the family. They have months to prepare and plan for the new addition. Unfortunately, transitioning into an emptier nest is much more abrupt. One day your child is at home, and suddenly that child moves away. It might take you ten to twelve months to adjust to your new normal, but just like the birth of a child, it will come in its own time.

 LIVING A FULL LIFE

- Have you considered creating a projected one-year calendar to chronicle your emotions and activities as you consider what to expect in your empty nest?
- How do you fill your day when you are alone?
- What would you do if you had the flexibility and freedom to commit to your day?

Chapter 6
Essential Workers

———•———

es·sen·tial (/əˈsen(t)SHəl/)

Adjective

1. absolutely necessary; extremely important.

   "it is essential to keep up-to-date records"

2. fundamental or central to the nature of something or someone.

   "the essential weakness of the plaintiff's case"

3. medicine (of a disease) with no known external stimulus or cause; idiopathic. "essential hypertension"

Noun

plural noun: essentials

1. a thing that is absolutely necessary.[3]

During the Coronavirus Pandemic of 2020, we became familiar with a descriptive category of people in the workforce. The term essential worker became an important part of the American vocabulary. Since the Coronavirus was thought to be extremely contagious, with no proven effective treatment or cure (at the time), governmental leaders around the world issued orders for most people to stay at home to stop, or at least slow down, the spread of this deadly virus. A separation system was established to identify those who would need to stay at home and work, and those who needed to continue to physically show up at their place of business.

WHO IS ESSENTIAL?

Those individuals in the second category were employed in certain vocations; deemed "essential." Those considered to be essential were most people in the medical community, public safety officials like police and fire, people who delivered packages, UPS, FedEx, grocery store employees, restaurant workers who could prepare takeout, and food delivery workers of various kinds. The list included those individuals who keep us safe, healthy, fed, and in the loop with our communication. Members of the media were also considered essential.

WHO IS UNESSENTIAL?

Those folks considered unessential were mandated to stay home. Some employees in this category could work from home; others were required to either take time off or be laid off. Not only was there a financial setback for someone classified as unessential there was an emotional price for anyone placed in that category. Some employees worked at jobs or in a career field for years, only to be told they were unessential. Perhaps that happened to you, or a loved one.

As a member of the media, I felt fortunate to continue working even as my heart broke for friends and family members who lost jobs or were forced to go on furlough. I couldn't help but think we were *all* essential.

In a way, the empty nester can fall into the category of feeling unessential. In the grand scheme of things, the contributions of parents are a necessary and vital part of an adult child's life. But on a day-to-day basis, a parent who no longer has a child living at home becomes a little less essential. The parent of an independent child no longer has the responsibility for tending to their child's daily needs, like preparing food or doing laundry.

Parents can slip into feelings of being irrelevant, but this isn't true. Every parent is essential; we just need to recognize the shift in *why* we are still essential. An adult child needs a parent to be encouraging and supportive, providing guidance and wisdom as that child makes important decisions about the future. As children enter the Young Adult season and make decisions about future education, starting a career, buying a house, or getting married, the supportive parent becomes a trusted advisor. To that end, the parent becomes *more* essential than perhaps any other time in a child's life.

 ## LIVING A FULL LIFE

- When it comes to your role in the life of your children who no longer live at home, what makes you feel unessential?
- Even though you are not involved in the day-to-day routine for your adult child, what are the things you do for your child that are essential?
- Are there places in your life where you are considered essential?

BIRDS OF A FEATHER (FRIENDSHIPS)

———

A friend is one that knows you as you are, understands where you have been, accepts what you have become, and still, allows you to grow.
William Shakespeare

Chapter 1
Circle Of Friends

———•———

*We have three types of friends in life: Friends for a reason,
friends for a season and friends for a lifetime.*
Author Unknown

Friendships fall into many categories. Certain friends come and
go out of our lives in different stages and different settings. Some
friendships are new. Others are enduring.

I like to think of the blessings of friendships falling into many
C Categories:

Connection
Communication
Casual
Consistent
Community
Companionship
Compassion

Counsel
Commonality
Cheerleader

Even though friendships often play a significant role in our social life, friendships can also impact our health and well-being. According to research conducted by the Mayo Clinic, good friends are good for our health.[4] During the good times in life, friends help us find joy and celebrate the good times. Trusted friends are valuable in providing comfort and support during bad times. The most special friends are the people we can't wait to share our good news and cry during times of sadness, loss, and pain. Friends keep us company, prevent loneliness and allow us to do the same for them.

Friends can also:

- Increase our sense of belonging and purpose.
- Boost our happiness and reduce stress.
- Improve our self-confidence and self-worth.
- Help us cope with traumas, such as divorce, serious illness, job loss, or the death of a loved one.
- Encourage us to change or avoid unhealthy lifestyle habits, such as excessive drinking or lack of exercise.[5]

As Dionne Warwick famously sang in her 1980s hit song, "That's What Friends Are For," friends are there for us for the long haul.

SEASONAL FRIENDS

One of my daughter Jacqueline's youth hockey coaches, Coach Trapp, used to say, "Love hockey. Hate the people." I can't imagine he was serious, but this line is unforgettable.

Relationships formed when a youngster is on a team are unique and special. The child becomes a *teammate*. It is a brand-new social reality for parents, too. They form their own team of sorts. There is a common journey shared with those involved to give those players the best chance to develop at the given sport.

- There's a common goal: to win.
- There is a common enemy: the opponent.

It can be like a roller-coaster ride of sorts, with the full range of emotions. There is excitement and adrenaline involved in game time encounters, which can also produce disappointment, jealousy, sadness, and sometimes even heartbreak. Some of those relationships are negative and unpleasant, while most are cordial and casual.

FRIENDSHIP CYCLE

Whether or not you like them, the reality is many of those relationships conclude at the end of a season. After all, because the reason for the friendship was the team, as the season ends, so does the makeup of the team and the surrounding relationships.

This is part of a cycle of relationships that plays itself out repeatedly when our children are in youth sports and even in school sports. To maintain those friendships post-season, a significant amount of work goes into finding spare time to spend together.

Since those children often move on to a new activity or sport, a whole new set of parental relationships forms.

It is a journey that often becomes emotional, and for parents like me, highly addictive.

For those who have children who take their sport or other activity into college, the amount of travel and number of contests can create even stronger bonds with other teammates' parents.

Even so, at some point, those years conclude, marking the end of a deeper set of relationships. Those forced friendships that have been the social equivalent of an arranged marriage have ended. While we are happy to end some of those relationships, others have become deep, real, and lasting.

As we transition to the Empty Nest season, the activities that fill our schedules and lives can be those of our choosing. So too are the friendships. No longer are we forced to have most of our friendships chosen by proximity or team colors, or mutual mascots. This is the time in life when we can now make friends based on common interests *we adults* share.

Occasionally, our new life journey reconnects us for special but limited events, like the mom of one of Jacqueline's tennis teammates. Pat Geelhoed's daughter, Tina, was part of the State Championship tennis team with Jacqueline during their senior year of high school. In addition to being a fellow tennis mom, Pat is a gifted photographer who took all of my kids' high school senior pictures. When I needed an author headshot for this book, I could think of no better person to reach out to than Pat. Since this important photo shoot took place during the COVID shutdowns, I'm grateful for Pat's creativity (and editing skills) as we took the photo in my driveway while I was three months overdue for a haircut!

TURNING SEASONAL FRIENDSHIPS INTO PERENNIALS

There is a peace as we enter this next season with some of these other parents who have traveled this same journey with us. That's the case for one of the dearest relationships in my life to grow over our kids' commonality. Jen Dailey and I became fast friends as I stalked her to convince her daughter Maddie to join my daughter Jennifer's AAU basketball team. That was during our daughters' freshman year in high school. Maddie not only joined that AAU team, with our girls playing travel basketball together, they also played basketball at the same university. During high school and college, these girls became each other's rocks. The same description applied to the moms' relationships.

As our daughters emptied their lockers and college nests to move on to the next season of their lives, the rich history of shared experiences has cemented a lifetime bond and enduring friendship between these two moms that now transcends the girls and the games.

One of the other unique friendships that has grown deep roots is with a special friend I met on the fringe of high school sports. Jill is just a few years behind me in the journey to empty her nest, but also experienced a significant feeling of loss as her sons graduated from high school. As a football mom, Jill took the lead in organizing big team meals and enjoyed the limelight of being the mother of two superstars playing under the Friday Night Lights. She and I bonded over fundraising for high school sports and shared painful emotions as we both spent the final chapters in that exhilarating part of our children's life journey (and ourselves). We have now become cheerleaders for each other as we transition into focusing more fully on our own lives and careers, but still enjoy walking down memory lane together. We enjoy reliving the glory days of our children now that the cheering has ended, and the bright lights are shining on the next class of high school athletes.

LIVING A FULL LIFE

- How would you describe the seasonal friendships that developed around your child(ren) and their activities?
- Does it make it harder to create lasting friendships because so many of them have been fleeting?
- How can you transform a seasonal friendship into a perennial friendship?

Chapter 8
Bobbers And Anchors

———•———

People inspire you or they drain you. Pick them wisely.

Hans F. Hansen

There is a series of TV shows on Bravo TV® called *The Real Housewives.* The shows feature groups of women in several major cities.

The show started in Orange County, California, promoted as a reality show that would chronicle the relationships and life adventures of a group of high-profile, incredibly wealthy, and successful women who are friends or in the same circle of friends.

Some individual relationships are closer than others, with some women in the group only acquaintances of one another and others being close friends.

From the initial show in the Los Angeles area, the series spread to include many different communities across the country, featuring high-profile, successful women in each location.

As of 2019, more than a dozen cities feature Real Housewives shows, from The Real Housewives of New York City to The Real Housewives of Beverly Hills, The Real Housewives of New Jersey, The Real Housewives of Atlanta, and even The Real Housewives of Salt Lake City. There are International versions of the shows from Vancouver to Melbourne to Athens. Lots of glamour, money, and drama.

Even though marketed and promoted as reality TV, it is difficult to believe genuine relationships would contain the explosive emotional drama and fireworks as those chronicled on these programs. It's my experience that real friendships don't meltdown into public screaming matches, name-calling, or back-biting that take center stage during each episode.

FRIENDS OR FRENEMIES?

I couldn't imagine behaving in such a way toward people, and not people who are in my social group or friend group.

As the shows continue season by season, these women have cameras following the group going through many extremes in their lives.

Some are getting married, some divorced, some are having babies, some are watching as their children grow up and move away, some battle substance abuse, and some are arrested.

Through these challenging times in life, when it would appear these women need a good friend's support, these relationships don't always showcase in a positive light what it means to be a loyal friend.

Of course, the ratings may not be as good if these women were having coffee, going to Bible study, playing cards or golf, and supporting one another in a positive way.

The drama continues, the cameras keep rolling, and millions of people watch it all unfold.

Perhaps it is best served as a cautionary tale for all of us who are in relationships with people, either casual or close. **How we treat people impacts how they think, act, and feel.** We have a real opportunity to treat others with kindness and compassion, and to be supportive and loving in every relationship in our lives.

REALITY? TV

While my sincere hope is that *The Real Housewives* are not displaying reality, there are valuable lessons to be learned regarding genuine friendship.

Indeed, no matter how much money someone has, how beautiful their home may be, or how glamorous they may appear, we each need to develop friendships that lift us instead of tearing us down. We are social creatures and can only be our best when we choose friendships and relationships that inspire us to be better versions of ourselves.

Indeed, the mark of character is how we behave when we believe nobody is watching, which might be why these women carry-on in such callous, dramatic and contemptuous ways in front of the camera.

Those relationships could only survive if there is true love, caring, and compassion when the bright lights stop shining.

LIVING A FULL LIFE

- Do you have friends or frenemies? Consider the Empty Nest season as a great time to end toxic relationships, even those that have lasted years or decades.
- How are your closest friends like-minded and supportive of you?
- Which friends can you rely on to keep your secrets and confidences? How can you serve those friends this week?

Chapter 9

A Friend in Need
is a Friend Indeed

———•———

Life is either a daring adventure or nothing at all.
Helen Keller

Have you ever struck up a conversation with someone just to pass the time in some random situation, only to realize later that it was a divine encounter?

That happened to me in 2015. **It happened at a funeral, of all places!**

FRIENDS PROVIDE COUNSEL

My husband runs a nonprofit organization with a dedicated board of directors. When one of the longtime members of the board passed away, a man who had helped shape the overall trajectory of my husband's organization, the funeral was well-attended. We got there early to get a good seat.

We walked in the door and took a seat next to one of my husband's long-term employees, Ann Webb. Ann is a valuable member of my husband's executive team, a woman I have known and admired for many years. She was already an empty nester, as her two children had graduated college and were making their way in the world in their careers.

As we waited for the funeral service to begin, my friend shared a conversation she had recently had with her daughter, Kristin. After college, Kristin took a job working at the Veterans Administration Hospital in California, with great benefits and stability working for a government organization.

Ann was upset and dismayed as she told me Kristin was thinking about quitting her job and taking a clerical position at a research facility in Antarctica.

LOOKING FOR SUPPORT

I think Ann was hoping I would agree with her opinion that to quit a reliable and stable job in sunny Southern California to take a position in Antarctica would be a terrible idea. Perhaps Ann hoped I would agree that Kristin was squandering the wonderful and reliable opportunity she had with her governmental job. Instead, I could only offer her a perspective that differed from the one she was considering.

I suggested she give Kristin her blessing and encourage her to follow this dream. I may have sounded like I was reciting a chapter in a self-help book, but I reminded her we only have one chance to live this life, and settling for the stable and routine can, in the short term, bring us a feeling of peace. But ten, twenty, or thirty years from now, we might look back and wonder about the path we didn't choose to take.

YOU ONLY LIVE ONCE (YOLO)

I found it ironic that we were having this conversation while waiting for a *funeral* to begin.

As her mother, Kristin was going to need Ann's support and encouragement in this adventure. There would be times when Kristin would be filled with doubt and second-guess herself. Still, from her mom's more experienced place in life, she needed Ann to be the voice of reassurance. There would always be an opportunity for Kristin to get another stable and traditional job.

An opportunity to travel the world, especially to experience life in Antarctica, would set Kristin apart from almost every other person she would meet in her life. She would have countless stories, memories, and experiences that would be more exciting and vivid than almost any movie she could ever watch at the local theater. Immediately after leaving the funeral, Ann called her daughter to share the breaking news of a sudden change of heart and offer Kristin her blessing for the journey. "It was freeing when I just 'let go' of my fight to convince her not to go! I couldn't wait to call her and give her my support," said Ann. "I couldn't wait another minute! I had to break the tension I had created between us because I wouldn't accept and respect her decision! It was like a weight lifted off my shoulders."

THE JOURNEYS OF MY CHILDREN

My perspective came from the journeys my children have taken.

When my son Jacob graduated from high school, he took a study trip to Israel for a few weeks. Organized by one of his high school hockey coaches, it was a trip he would take with his coach, a couple of friends, and a bunch of strangers. It would not be a family trip. His father and I would not be joining in the adventure. Up to this point in his life, Jacob's only trips away from home were to sports camps and Young Life Summer Camp.

I worried about him the entire time he was gone, but when he returned, he was full of joy and enthusiasm when sharing his experiences with all of us. His trip through the Holy Land brought the Bible and all the teachings he had studied growing up to life. No longer did he have to rely on his imagination when he read the words of scripture. He had seen those places and walked in the same steps!

Just a couple years later, while he was a college student, Jacob went back to Israel to study for an entire semester in Jerusalem. I could see the transformation and impact in his life. As newlyweds, Jacob and his wife Taylor returned to Israel for another round of educational experiences. They explored the country and culture while Jacob audited a few more courses at Jerusalem University. Taylor volunteered to help care for special needs children at a program in Bethlehem.

A few years later, my daughter Jacqueline went with a medical mission group to Africa. The following year, she and her husband became missionaries and spent a few months serving people in Africa. They worked with people in Ethiopia and at an orphanage and missionary hospital in South Sudan before visiting with missionaries in Uganda. While I was nervous about them being gone, I knew their experiences would be game changers in their lives moving forward!

As I was encouraging my friend to call her daughter and give her mother's blessing for her planned life-changing mission, I told her there would be something liberating about giving her daughter the support to go on this adventure. Even the fact Kristin was asking for her mother's blessing to follow this dream meant Ann's opinion was still important, which is a significant compliment to an empty nest parent. Ann points to the decision to support Kristin as transformational in their adult parent-child relationship. "Antarctica really has been a blessing as it allows me to spend so much more time with Kristin, and it helped shape her into the adventurous and principled woman she is today!"

By the way, one of the unexpected by-products of my children going on their adventures was a significant increase in communication and connection we shared while they were so far away.

Thanks to the Internet and communication apps, I received updates and stayed in touch almost more than when my kids were on their college campuses in my backyard.

As parents, we must give our kids roots *and* wings! And we must encourage our friends to provide their children the same, especially if we have already walked a mile in the shoes they are about to put on!

 ## LIVING A FULL LIFE

- How do you respond when your child wants to go on a life-changing adventure?
- How do you encourage and voice support for your child to follow a dream?
- How can you help your friends encourage and interact with their children?

Chapter 10
My Accidental Life Coach

—•—

A life coach does for the rest of your life what a personal trainer
does for your health and fitness.

Elaine MacDonald, The Coaching Tools Company

As part of my profession as an on-air television personality, I frequently receive invitations to serve as speaker or emcee for events. Often, the individual who is reaching out to schedule an appearance only knows me as the person they see on television. The relationship I have with that individual typically involves spending just a few hours of my time helping with their event.

I am always honored to receive an invitation to be a part of the program and am flattered an organization would want my assistance in guiding its special event.

The flow includes exchanging emails with the organizer of the event so we can be on the same page in terms of the tone and feel of the event, along with a rundown of the schedule of activities.

I have done so many of these throughout the years that a phone conversation and series of e-mails is typically the extent of the advanced preparation. The organizer sends me an e-mail of the program and any special notes I need to review in advance, then we have a brief face-to- face conversation when I arrive at the venue for the event.

A couple years ago, I received such a request. The Chamber of Commerce in the community where I live was celebrating its twentieth anniversary. The organization's executive director reached out to me to be the emcee for this milestone celebration. The event was a luncheon, recognizing its growth and importance, as well as honoring many of the individuals and businesses that had helped it survive and thrive for those two decades. My part of the event would be simple; welcome the attendees, introduce a few speakers and a special video presentation, and interview a few of the organization's key members. When I emcee events, I view my role as a combination cruise director and air traffic controller. I guide audience members through the program and keep everything going on schedule.

Since this was a special event in my very own community, the organizer and I made a special appointment to meet ahead of time to review the rundown of activities for the event over a glass of wine at a local restaurant.

That initial meeting was the beginning of one of the most amazing new friendships in my life. Amy was the Executive Director of the Byron Center Chamber of Commerce. Not only was the event celebrating the twenth-year milestone of the Byron Center Chamber, but it was also marking Amy's separation from the organization, as she was leaving to become a staff member at a local life coach organization.

Amy was smart and funny, and we discovered we had similar personalities. She was in a similar life stage; her three sons were grown and had started down their career paths. (Two of her adult sons lived at home, so her nest was full and empty at the same time.)

In the months following the Chamber event, Amy started working at her new organization, going through the certification to become a life coach.

I became her very first client. Actually, you could call me a guinea pig as she was using me to test out the material she learned. As we went through my evaluation, I shared the difficult space I was in emotionally in my life. By this time, she knew about the tailspin I was in as I transitioned into life as an empty nester.

As we discussed the challenges I was facing, she helped me make a significant discovery. Amy helped me figure out certain times of the day that were much more difficult for me than others. The most challenging time of the day was the early to mid-afternoon time frame when I was done with my workday but didn't have anybody relying on me. Through the life coaching exercises, Amy helped me connect the feelings of sadness and emptiness with the lack of a short-term purpose.

Not only did we identify the difficult time frame, but Amy also helped me recognize the importance of filling my schedule (at least a few days a week) with activities or appointments during those critical hours in the early afternoon. Indeed, part of the remedy for my feelings of melancholy and loneliness was to fill those hours with activities. This strategy helped pull me out of the emotional low I was often feeling.

It's interesting to think I would never have actively sought the service of a life coach, but what a blessing for me that a new friendship would come with the unique expertise, perspective, and insight of such a warm and caring person.

 ## LIVING A FULL LIFE

- Are there certain times of the day that are more emotionally difficult for you than others?
- Have you ever considered talking to a life coach or trained counselor for perspective?
- Who are the friends who can help you get a new perspective on life's difficulties?

Chapter 11
Literary Friends

———•———

I kept always two books in my pocket, one to read, one to write in.
Robert Louis Stevenson

Different people come into our lives in different seasons, especially as we transition from one stage in life to another. With the free time I discovered in the Empty Nest season, I became determined to reach for a dream I'd been harboring for at least four decades, the dream to write a book. I'm in good company with this dream as an article by Justine Tal Goldberg[6] on the website Publishing Perspectives. The article presents research by Joseph Epstein that suggests eighty-one percent of Americans want to write a book.

That's two hundred *million* people!

Why don't more people write that book? Perhaps it's a lack of time, ambition, confidence, or know-how. I used many of those perceived barriers as excuses for why I had not chased my literary dream. Like many want-to-be authors, I had talked about my goal so often that for Christmas one year, my son Jacob and daughter-in-law Taylor bought me the specialized author software package Scrivener[7] for my home computer!

So how did I turn that decades-long dream into the pages you are reading? By creating a literary tribe. I'm so grateful for a group of extraordinary people who have come into my life over the past several years. They have helped mentor and inspire me as I reached for my dream of becoming a published author.

MY FIRST AUTHOR FRIEND

God brings certain people into our lives to serve as special inspirations and Cindy Bultema is that person in my life. I got to know Cindy a couple years ago when she stepped away from her successful career as an author, speaker, and thought leader in the women's Christian inspirational space, to take over the role as executive director for an important Christian ministry for young girls called GEMS. GEMS stands for Girls Everywhere Meeting the Savior. *I'm thinking about lobbying Cindy to start a similar organization for empty nesters called Grandparents Everywhere Meeting the Savior.*

Cindy and I connected as she was taking over her new role. She asked me to help with some remarkable new initiatives she was starting within this organization. Interestingly, my daughters had both been GEMS growing up, and I was even a GEMS leader in our church at one point. My meeting with Cindy was one where we talked about this great organization and where I could pick her brain about her life as an author and speaker.

I shared my lifelong desire to become an author, and she became a wonderful mentor and prayer partner as she helped encourage me to reach for my dream.

It would take me a couple years to gain the confidence to start writing my first book. Still, occasional meetings with Cindy gave me the motivation and inspiration I needed to believe I had an important message to share with women walking through the same stage in life I was experiencing.

Cindy's important message to me was that she wrote books aimed at helping women through different times in their lives; many were Christian devotional books. Her life as a speaker allowed her to travel to conferences and workshops and serve as a teacher, counselor, coach, and cheerleader. Cindy's career was similar to the one I had been envisioning for me.

In her new role as GEMS leader, she also incorporated those wonderful aspects of her life and creativity into breathing life, new life into this crucial worldwide ministry.

I think God for putting her into my life. As a member of my tribe, I value her prayer support and wisdom as I enter this new chapter of my own life. She was the very first member of my prayer team as I signed a contract for the book you're reading.

I often look back and think about those special people who have come into my life over the last couple of years, at a time when I am changing when my life can seem empty.

Friends like Cindy have important perspectives for us. They help us understand that even though our nest is empty, there is a full life waiting. Like me, you may be inspired to become an inspiration for other women.

A "NOVEL" FRIENDSHIP

I first met Tracy Brogan, ironically, when she was in our studio to research a novella she was writing. She was doing behind the scenes research about the inner workings of a television station. One of her principal characters was a meteorologist who was working in the world of morning television. She came into the television station to job shadow, and we clicked.

She writes romances and romantic comedies. Her first book has sold over one million copies worldwide, and she has had several more highly successful titles since then. In fact, she recently crossed the lifetime sales benchmark of three million books sold!

I found Tracy to be an inspiration because she had harbored dreams of becoming an author for many years before taking the leap to submit her first manuscript. She believed in herself enough to send the manuscript and take a giant leap. She made me think I could do the same.

Tracy is also a divorced mother of two girls and entering the Empty Nest season. Her oldest daughter is already a college student. Her youngest graduated from high school during the Coronavirus Pandemic of 2020 and moved away to college.

FROM INTERVIEW TO INSPIRATION

It has been more than a decade since Wade Rouse fanned my literary fire. He had walked away from a lucrative career to make writing his full-time occupation. As a guest on the eight-West couch, Wade's appearance was to promote his memoir *It's All Relative*. At the time, I found it amazing that a successful Random House-contracted author lived in Saugatuck, just one county away from me in West Michigan. Over the past decade, Wade has become a mentor and encourager, as he has written more best-selling novels under the pen name Viola Shipman (to honor his late grandmother). Wade's willingness to share his expertise and enthusiasm has led me to believe that I could become an author. One of the most significant pieces of advice I received from Wade was the secret to successfully finishing the writing process, "Keep your butt in the seat!" Wade's advice was clever and funny, but a guiding truth as I have worked to create this book. To actually finish something, I had to *sit down* and *do the work*!

LITERARY PART-TIMERS

A few other members of my literary tribe have written (or helped produce) books as they continued with successful careers. I'll never forget the admiration (and envy) I felt when people I KNEW had written and published books.

Cynthia: I was in the library and found the book *Small Business for Big Thinkers* staring at me. It was written by a woman I knew, Cynthia Kay, who was a communications expert with a successful video production, coaching, and event production business.

Rick: I was on vacation in Florida and opened my iPad to review e-mails and discovered a request from Rick Vuyst to write an endorsement to be included in his first book, *I Just Wet my Plants*. Rick ran a successful group of landscaping stores called Flowerland, and had become the go-to expert for all things plants, landscaping, and flowers in West Michigan. Rick's green thumb and quick wit served him well as the host of a weekly radio show focused on helping people with their planting dilemmas.

Tommy: With a last name synonymous with great value in a steak dinner, Tommy Brann put the lessons he learned from a lifetime spent in the difficult restaurant industry into a book called *Mind Your Own Business/Lessons from a Hardworking Restauranteur*.

Ginger: The honest life-lessons from a former co-worker who has become a nationwide household name. Ginger Zee's New York Times Best-Selling Memoir, *Natural Disasters: I Cover Them I Am One*, is a candid and inspirational journey through Ginger's battle with mental health issues, substance abuse, and an abusive relationship. She is one of the most recognizable and respected people in America. Ginger has also written a series of adventure books for young girls designed to entertain and spark an interest in meteorology.

Tim: The former Grand Valley State University Athletic Director who turned this rural West Michigan college into a perennial NCAA Division II powerhouse, Tim Selgo penned *Competitive Greatness the Grand Valley Way*, before stepping away from the GVSU Athletic Department to become an inspirational speaker, leader, and coach.

As I considered launching my literary career, I wondered how each of these people had written books and had them published! So, I reached out to each of these individuals for advice and counsel. While each author had a different journey, genre, and audience, the message I received from each of them was the same: *Just go for it*!

IT'S ALL ABOUT THE EDITING

My final two special relationships are with the unsung heroes (and heroines) of the publishing world: the editors. Andy Rogers was my initial material and developmental editor, who helped take a bunch of words, thoughts, and ideas and sculpt them into a manuscript that began to look (and read) like an actual *book*!

Tricia McDonald has edited, produced, and published multiple books over the decades. I was introduced to this literary dynamo by another of my author friends, Rick Vuyst, when changing publishing houses from one that provided all of the editing services for its signed authors to one that required authors to hand in fully edited manuscripts. Since Tricia is also a member of the Empty Nest Club, she provided a double-dose of expertise. I cannot imagine this book having the same impact without her insight and oversight.

I'm so grateful to have these special people in my life, as they have been instrumental in inspiring me to launch my literary career. They have inspired me and helped me gain the courage to work on my book. So even though our encounters and initial meetings were coincidental, the relationships we have developed are true blessings.

Writing a book is a difficult undertaking. Whether you write a book someday or not, you will be challenged by something new. Having trusted friends and advisors who have gone through this experience made it easier for me to navigate the hard times. Don't be afraid to seek out people who will help you navigate new experiences. Developing personal relationships with people who have already accomplished the dreams you have for yourself will make those goals seem more do-able. Since writing a book had been a dream of mine for decades, I tended to put published authors on a pedestal. Getting to meet and become friends with these people who had already accomplished that milestone (many times over) made my dream seem possible. A relationship with an actual person, in the flesh, might just be a significant first step in your journey to reach a major life goal.

 LIVING A FULL LIFE

- Who are the people in your life who help to nurture and support you?
- Are there people you could reach out to who are already accomplishing the dreams or goals you have for yourself?
- Where could you find a person to help point you on the road to reaching your dream? Consider joining a club or finding a network of successful people in the field you are considering and those who, like you, are just starting.

Chapter 12
Enduring Friendships

———•———

Close friends are truly life's treasures. Sometimes they know us
better than we know ourselves. With gentle honesty, they are there
to guide and support us, to share our laughter and our tears. Their
presence reminds us that we are never really alone.

Vincent van Gogh

We all have certain people in our lives who have been there for
decades. Those are enduring friendships. For me, these friendships
evolved in a variety of ways. In my life, I can point to four friendships that have each crossed the two-decade mark.

PHYSICIAN HEAL . . . THY FRIEND

Dr. Renee is one of the most accomplished and popular OB/
GYNs in West Michigan and has become an important part of my
life. We were both pregnant when we met, she with her first and
me with my last. Now she's emptying her nest, too. Three of her

four birds have made lives of their own, two as college students, and one in law school. The youngest is a high schooler.

I treasure this friendship because we have walked so many of life's journeys together. We brought babies into the world within a few months of each other and experienced the journey of life of those two special babies.

LEGAL AID

Kris is an attorney who specializes in family law. Our friendship began because both of our husbands would spend tons of their free time on the golf course, leaving us as young moms to fill our free time. When the kids were younger, some of those days would be spent hanging out for hours by the pool. As the kids got older and busier, and hours at the pool time was no longer an option, our friendship strengthened. Now that we are empty nesters, live nearby, and often have the same schedule for alone time, Kris is a great friend for regular companionship. Plus, we are new members of the Grandma Club, so it's a blessing to have a trusted friend who is navigating this new role in my life with me.

BONDING ON THE BOARD

My relationship with Christy grew out of our shared passion to create programs to address our community's significant mental health issues. Christy is the Executive Director of the Mental Health Foundation of West Michigan. Our friendship began after I started volunteering. I eventually assumed a leadership role as president of the Board of Directors, which gave us even more opportunities to connect and work together. We share a similar life journey, each with three active children and busy careers. Our youngest daughters even played travel soccer together for a brief season. As we enter the Empty Nest season, we rely on each other for support and encouragement. We are helping each other navigate the current challenges in life while finding fun memories in the past and looking ahead to the promise of the future. Christy is now joining the Grandma Club, so I'm excited to help her celebrate this next season in life.

NEIGHBORLY LOVE

My final enduring friendship evolved through proximity and children, as our oldest boys played baseball together, locally and in a travel league. Our youngest daughters, born within a few months of each other, have grown up alongside each other. They are closer than many girls, closer even than most sisters. LuAnn and I have been neighbors for nearly two decades, and have watched each other's kids grow up, get married, graduate from college, and have families of their own. LuAnn joined the Grandma Club multiple times before I was blessed with my very first grandchild, so I was fortunate to have her walk me into this new season of my life. We have watched parents grow old, enter nursing homes, and eventually pass away.

Enduring friendships are relationships that evolve. These special bonds have been nurtured through decades of doing life together. We know the stories of each other's lives because we have lived them *together*. The life journey of each of our children, our relationships with our spouses, and our parents have played out with each other in real-time.

NO WORDS NEEDED

Our life stories need no explanation. We share perspectives that are real and honest and could never be captured fully by just explaining them to someone. Enduring friendships have to be *lived.* They take time, and through the time and struggles, they grow into some of the most precious relationships of all.

And now, as we each travel this next stretch of life's journey together, we all know the history and memories that have made each of us who we are today: the laughter and tears—the celebrations and disappointments. There is no replacing these amazing friendships that have stood the test of time.

We used to think the most challenging season was the Juggling Act when our kids were growing up. Kris has two kids, I have my three, Renee has four kids, Christy has three, and Lu has six! But we are all discovering the Empty Nest season is an even more challenging time of life.

THE COMING YEARS

This season of life will be filled with emotions of significant extremes. We will walk through the next two or three decades together as we celebrate more marriages, arrivals of additional grandchildren, and sadly, mourn special people's passing in our lives, which is bound to happen.

With deep history, enduring friendships will allow us to walk confidently through this next stage, secure in the relationships we've built. It is with complete confidence that enduring friends know we have each other and will always be there for each other as the journey of life continues to unfold.

LIVING A FULL LIFE

- Who are your enduring friends?
- Consider the importance of these relationships that are filled with history and hope and promise. What can you do for or with these friends this week?
- As you empty the nest, do you spend more time with friends in your same life stage?

Chapter 13
Four-Legged Friends

———●———

I have found that when you are deeply troubled, there are things that you get from the silent devoted companionship of a dog that you can get from no other source.

Doris Day

I'm the first to admit I have never been a pet person. Especially not a dog person. While they were growing up, my kids would often beg me to get them a dog. The answer was always "no" for a variety of reasons:

- The nest was already full.
- The Juggling Act season seemed too overwhelming to even entertain the thought of getting a dog.
- Dogs are a lot of work!
- They are smelly and dirty.

- A dog can damage a house and leave hair (and other messy things) behind.
- Dogs also need companionship, and we were out of the house so much of the time.

I was *not* a dog person—until Hank came along.

My daughter Jenn adopted Hank after she graduated from college. She was looking for a companion and was encouraged by a dog-loving friend to get a dog. I did not support this idea, but since she was a grown-up college graduate living outside the home, I did not have a say in this plan. I was also less than enthusiastic because Hank was not just a tiny puppy. He is half Great Dane/half mastiff-Lab and considered a giant breed dog. To put it simply: full-grown Hank would easily weigh more than me!

Maybe you can see where this furry relationship is going. I have fallen in love with that dog. Hank is big, but sweet. Occasionally, Jenn needs a pet sitter and asks me to watch him for a few hours, or to head over to her apartment and take him for a walk or let him out to go potty.

As my relationship with Hank has grown (I now call him my "grand dog"), I have realized the great potential of having a four-legged friend to help fill the empty nest.

An article by Kristen Sturt pointed out ten health benefits of having a dog, including improved heart health, boosting fitness and activity levels, improving your social life, reducing stress, helping to stave off depression, helping to lose weight, and adding to a feeling of purpose. [8] Pets are so important to mental health that organizations match former members of the military with animals. Pets for Vets [9] and Pets for Patriots [10] encourage pet adoption to provide a veteran with the companionship, responsibility, and love that comes from adopting a four-legged friend.

Having a pet can also help expand your social circle. With Hank around, I discovered the community that surrounds pet owners. This canine community includes fresh and friendly encounters at dog parks and along walking trails. People who have dogs are passionate about their animals and typically love meeting others with the same feelings. Adding a dog to your empty nest can give you a sense of purpose and increase your social circle all at once.

If you are looking to add energy and a sense of purpose to your empty nest, perhaps a trip to the pet store or local animal shelter might be something to consider. I have given thought to getting a dog to help fill my empty nest, but having Hank in my life is almost like having another grandchild. I can enjoy him as much as I want, but when he needs to go potty in the middle of the night, it's Jenn who gets to take him out!

 ## LIVING A FULL LIFE

- If you have a pet, how has it helped you transition to the empty nest?
- If you don't have a pet, how do you think it could help fill your nest (and life)?
- Can you think about people in your life who have a dog and might benefit from having your help in caring for their pet when life is busy for them?

Chapter 14
On Golden Nest

———•———

Age is an issue of mind over matter.
If you don't mind, it doesn't matter.
Mark Twain

There is a great blessing in finding older friends. In this special season in life, as we reach out to new friendships and relationships, it's a blessing to connect to people in our lives who have already been through this transitional stage.

I'm fortunate to be part of a social community, specifically a golf course community, where many of the people I have connected with through my twenty-plus years of membership are ahead of me in life by at least a decade. It has been fantastic to watch as these women emptied their nests and have navigated through some of life's joyous and arduous journeys.

GOLF BUDDIES

My husband and I have become closest friends with an older couple at our golf course, Dave and Margo, following a surprise invitation to Dave's retirement party. He had been a successful leader of a corporation, so his company was throwing a retirement dinner. We were honored to be among the guests because even though we were friends through the golf course, we weren't necessarily in the inner circle of his more senior group. Most of the people in that group had been successful in their careers and reached the stage of retirement. Many members of this flock were building new nests as they were flying south for the winter, downsizing their homes, and becoming grandparents, basically walking the path we all would walk one day.

The invitation to the retirement dinner triggered a new friendship that developed over the next few years, taking annual trips to visit them in Florida during the cold winter months to play golf and just get away for a few days. These invitations started when my kids were all still living at home, so I surprised myself by accepting those invitations. I had a tough time away from my kids during those years, feeling like I always needed to be available when or if they needed something from me.

Since they had already emptied their original nest (with their sons getting married and having children), Margo and Dave had already walked the path we are walking now. Somehow, watching them survive and even *thrive* in this new season of life was reassuring and gave me a sense of peace, hope, and excitement. Our special friendship continued to strengthen as our kids graduated from high school, went to college, got married, and made us grandparents.

NINETY IS THE NEW SIXTY

Besides my more seasoned friends at the golf course, I also discovered an extraordinary friendship with a man who is less than a decade away from reaching the century mark. I met Buck Matthews when I interviewed him for our morning show, eightWest, after he published his first book. We struck an immediate bond, as he had been a weatherman and talk show host at my television station years before. We often joke that he is me without the high heels or lipstick.

Since Buck had already written his first book, I leaped at the chance to meet him for lunch and discuss the process of becoming a published author. Our first lunch lasted for two hours and I was hooked on this friendship.

Buck was the first person I allowed to read any of the words I had written. He became a writing coach and encouraged, inspired and challenged me to take the leap of faith in writing this book. Indeed, without his encouragement, I probably never would have found the courage within myself to even reach out for the first appointment.

Looking around our world at older people provides a great field of friendships. The best friendships are two-way streets. We give, and we get. Who is someone older you could *give* something to?

Friendships with older people allows us to gain wisdom and valuable perspective from their experiences. In turn, we allow them to serve as a mentor, while we both enjoy great conversation and companionship; two things often missing in the empty nest.

LIVING A FULL LIFE

- Do you have friends who are older than you and in the next stage in life?
- How do you think you will benefit from developing relationships with people in the next stage in life?
- In which area of your life could an older friend serve as a mentor?

Chapter 15
Virtual Friendships

———•———

Friendship is born at that moment when one person says to the other, "What! You too? I thought I was the only one."

C. S. Lewis

It's one thing to pour your heart out to your friends or people you know about the turmoil of the Empty Nest season, but what about making connections with a bunch of strangers?

SOCIAL NEST-WORKING

I stumbled upon a Facebook community for empty nesters, called The Empty Nesters Community, and was immediately drawn in. The community describes itself as a "Support and Helping Community for empty nesters and those preparing for the empty nest to talk openly about the good, the exciting and the overwhelming of the empty nest." [11] The members of this group share the sadness, emptiness, and challenges that are a big part of this new season in life. The words written in those posts were so hauntingly familiar. In post after post, message after message, comment after comment, conversation after conversation, I felt as though someone had implanted a word processor into my brain to allow my very own thoughts and feelings to leap onto the page.

Sharon Hodor Greenthal is the creator of this Facebook group. She is a talented writer and blogger on parenting and family topics. She began writing about the Empty Nest season a few years ago. She has built her own tribe and is authentically sharing the space with thousands of people all over the country who are now connecting because of her vision and insight.

I reached out to Sharon for the backstory of the Facebook group. She told me she started the community in early 2016.

"I had been writing about empty nesting and parenting young adults for six years, and I was looking for inspiration for content for both my freelance work and the column I wrote for *The Spruce* on Parenting Young Adults (I no longer write that column). My friends Lisa Heffernan and Mary Dell Harrington, who are the founders of Grown and Flown, had started a FB group for parents of college students, and I thought this would be a good way to focus on the parents vs. the kids. [12]

"It grew very quickly. There are spikes in members joining each year in July/August when kids go off to college. I have done no recruiting or marketing; it's all been word of mouth. As one of my friends said, this is my philanthropic work. I spend a lot of time managing the community with the help of one admin, and it can be challenging."

I asked Sharon what her most significant surprise discovery was in the Facebook community, and she said, "The biggest surprise to me is the deep pain so many people experience when their kids leave home. Personally, while my friends and I felt a sense of loss, we moved on with our lives and found new ways to spend our time (for example, I started my blog). But in this group, there are some very sad people. I do think this is sort of self-selecting, though if you are a happy empty nester, you probably aren't looking for a support group."

FRIENDS AVAILABLE 24/7

Discovering groups of other empty nesters on social media is a great way to connect people in similar situations who are available any time of the day or night. These are people who may be dealing with or have dealt with what you may be facing. It is cathartic, reassuring, and uplifting to discover that no matter what the issue, someone else and indeed many others are going through the same thing.

 LIVING A FULL LIFE

- Challenge yourself to expand your virtual friendships. Try joining a Facebook group or other social media group related to the Empty Nest season. How would you find comfort in reading stories from others who feel the same thing you do?
- What could you (or would you) share with a new virtual friend that would encourage them?
- Consider STARTING a social media group, so you could develop questions and topics for timely and topical conversations to encourage engagement and connection. How would you find a purpose in that role?

THE ACTUAL NEST (HABITAT)

———

A house is made of walls and beams;
a home is made of hopes and dreams.
Unknown Author

Chapter 16
Is Your Nest A Shrine
Or A Museum?

———●———

There's no place like home.
Dorothy from *Wizard of Oz*

On a few occasions, we have considered the possibility of downsizing, so we invited realtors to look at our house to see what the value would be on the open market. The first piece of advice from each professional has been to de-personalize the house. We were told a potential buyer needs to have the vision of a blank canvas; what the space may look like if they were to buy it. Instead, our nest is covered with photographs throughout the years of our family. There are lots of family pictures; wedding pictures of the kids, family pictures from trips through the years, each child at different stages of life and development, and pictures from our family adventures along the way. Basically, my home style has been to create a shrine to the family.

And now that we have a grandchild, pictures of Levi are getting prominence in the family decoration scheme.

STYLE OF MEMORIES

Why decorate my home in this way? I love the memories of all those adventures. From our trip to Yellowstone and Grand Teton to Mackinac Island, to a remote fishing camp in Canada, and so much more. Those pictures represent the storyline of an incredible thirty years. There is also a feeling of familiarity and company that comes as those smiling faces look right back at me. Sometimes I stop and stare into the faces in those pictures and allow my mind to wander back to the precise moment when the image was captured.

When my nest first emptied, I would feel melancholy and sad to think so much of life was behind me.

SHIFTING FROM A SHRINE INTO A MUSEUM

It became clear I treated the décor of my home with reverence, fearing that changing any of these pictures would somehow negate (or even erase) the memories.

The Oxford Advanced Learner's Dictionary defines a shrine as "a place where people come to worship because it is connected with a holy person or event; or a place people visit because it is connected with someone or something that is important to them; containing memorabilia of a particular revered person or thing."[13] In my nest, I had built a shrine to the memories of years gone by. The photos were revered, on prominent display, and treated as if they religious artifacts—not to be moved or touched.

Instead of treating these photos as items to be honored and adored, I have shifted my mindset to treat these photographic displays of family memories more like displays in a museum. Those pictures capture history, not to be worshipped, but to be remembered!

ROTATING EXHIBITIONS

Nearly every museum has a series of different displays called exhibitions. There are exhibitions a museum owns and are always on display as part of their permanent collection. But to keep visitors engaged enough to return, a successful museum will also display items borrowed or purchased from other museums or agencies.

Building on that theme, the décor of an empty nester can also evolve and change throughout the year. My personal style includes swapping photos from the Juggling Act season with images from the Empty Nest season. This may comprise pictures of just myself and my husband, or photographs of me with my friends during memorable events. The new photo displays include my (now grown) children with their spouses, grandson, and even grand dog, pictures that don't even include me (gasp)!

Every piece of history a museum owns is valuable. Just because something isn't on displayed doesn't mean it isn't valued. The same is true for the displays in your home.

I have shifted my mindset to allow some photographs to be swapped out or replaced from time to time. As a result, I find it easier to enjoy the emotions when I look at these photos. The memories brought up bring me more joy than melancholy. Happy for the life we shared as a family . . . and excited for the new memories to come in the years ahead.

 ## LIVING A FULL LIFE

- What feelings do you fill with when you look at pictures of days-gone-by?
- Do you think about replacing some photographs? Why or why not?

- Would you describe your home as a shrine, museum, or something else?

Chapter 11
Do We Move To A New Nest?

———•———

Are you going to love it or are you going to list it?
Hilary Farr, David Visentin on *Love it or List It*

There is a television show I love called *Love It or List It*. Hilary Farr is a classy, talented interior designer, and David Visentin is a spunky, funny real estate agent. The two embark on an episode-by-episode competition to help families make decisions about their housing situations.

Each family profiled in an episode is no longer satisfied with their current house. In most cases, the house is too small or doesn't function properly, needing more than just an aesthetic makeover. So, the family has decided their nest is no longer the right fit. The family gives a designer a budget, a list of items, and spaces that need to be changed or improved for that house to continue to serve the family's needs in the present and into the future.

In most episodes, viewers learn the family moved into the house in a different life season. Gradually, year-by-year, circumstances changed. The family grew either by having more children or grew to need more space because they got older and bigger. The needs and tastes of the family changed for a variety of different reasons.

As the designer works through the list of changes, the home is transformed. One major thing that can't change is the square footage. The house is transformed into a more workable space, but the overall size remains the same. The other thing that can't change is the location of the home. In real estate, there's a phrase that says it's all about Location, Location, Location. No matter what the transformation is of the space, the location is what it is, for good or bad.

While the designer and construction team transform the family's home, the realtor takes the family on tours of potential new homes. He shows the family homes that are move-in ready dwellings and check all the boxes on the family's wish list. The new homes already have the right number of bedrooms and bathrooms, an updated kitchen, and often an open floor plan, along with perhaps the most suitable backyard or preferred garage. It is a turnkey solution to giving the family everything it has identified on that list of what they want in a living space. Sometimes, the new home is in a different neighborhood or a different location, which may or may not present an objection to the family. At the end of the journey, the family tours their current home, with all the renovations complete. At the end, the designer asks, "Are you going to love it?" while the realtor asks, "Are you going to list it?" Will the family stay put, or will the family pack up their boxes and move to that new space?

The decision becomes emotional along the way, especially for families looking to leave a home where they have been for many years and experienced significant life changes. Maybe they brought babies home from the hospital into that house, or it was their very first home. They may have watched their children grow up in that home. The attachment to the house is an essential part of the story.

As I have experienced the Empty Nest season shift, I have frequently thought about changing my nest. An emotional attachment to my surroundings often seems to be the deciding factor for considering moving or staying put. Maybe you feel this way, too. Moving out of the home where your children grew up feels like moving away from the memories. And while I don't believe in ghosts, I can close my eyes and picture my children opening presents under the tree in our great room on Christmas morning, bounding through the front door with excitement after making the Varsity team, or answering the door to find a high school crush on the front porch with the "prom-posal." Occupying the same space where these memories took place somehow keeps those memories alive and fresh.

But does it really?

As my time in our empty nest continues, I'm finding it easier to let go of the need to physically occupy the same space where all those incredible memories happened. Time has had a way of allowing me to focus on what I want. I have begun to reflect on a more personal list of questions about my living environment:

- Do I need all this space?
- Do I want to keep living in the same location?
- Would I prefer a smaller space?
- Do I want to live in a more urban setting?
- Would I prefer a condo or a house in this stage of life?

- Am I willing to keep spending as much time on the cleaning and upkeep of my nest?
- Would changing my living environment make it easier to focus on the future?

When I watch *Love it or List It*, I typically root for the people on the show to stay with their current (but now updated) home, mainly because of all the memories that happened there. As time in my own empty nest has marched on, I find it easier to imagine the benefits for the people on the program (and even myself) of making a different choice. Moving into a new nest does not erase the memories of the Juggling Act season. A move may even allow the making of fresh memories to come more easily.

By the way, one additional blessing will be the knowledge that another family will get to spend their Juggling Act years in the nest that was such a warm and comfortable place for raising your flock.

 ## LIVING A FULL LIFE

- What is keeping you in your current nest?
- When you consider where to live in the Empty Nest season, what are your priorities?
- Who comes to mind when you think about someone who could help you explore the decision about perhaps changing your nest? Reach out to that person for a conversation and start exploring your options. There's no harm in looking!

Chapter 18
Climate Change

—●—

When I no longer thrill to the first snow of the season,
I'll know I'm growing old.

Lady Bird Johnson

It's confession time. I hate cold weather. I dislike snow. I don't like ice.

The irony, of course, is that as a television meteorologist in a northern climate, I forecast snow and ice with a smile on my face! For a few short years when I was in preschool and kindergarten, my family lived in Missouri, not exactly the tropics, but at least warmer than across the northern states. So, aside from a brief stint during a part of my life I can barely remember, I have hopscotched across the northern part of the United States. I was born in New Jersey. After kindergarten, we moved to Montana. Of course, I did not have any say in that matter.

But the choices that followed were all me. I hopscotched across the country during my college years. From Montana, I moved west to attend Washington State University for two years. I then moved east to Wisconsin, where I finished my first degree in Wisconsin, and began my professional career. After a few years in Wisconsin, I took a position for a brief period in South Dakota before moving to Michigan to climb another rung on the television news ladder.

At each career crossroads, I had a decision to make about where to plant myself for the next chapter in my life. The television news business works a little like professional sports. You start by working in a smaller market to gain a year or two of experience and then move to a bigger market and then an even bigger market after that until you reach the network or a market where you decide to put down roots and live your life. This was the case back in the 1980s and 90s, though with today's world of online reporting and digital technology, moving up or down by several market sizes at a time is easier. Back then, to get a new position, a personality would make a videotape of several of their best segments and mail it to news directors where there was an opening. Applying at each station was an individual proposition, so a candidate could look for a position in any geographic area in the country.

NORTHERN GIRL

For me, living in a northern climate was almost all I had known. I applied at stations several hundred to a couple thousand miles away from where I was living (or where my parents were living). Yet, it seemed only logical for me to apply to television news jobs in the northern part of the United States.

When I took the position in Michigan, I did not know I would make this the final market stop in my career. I would spend the next thirty-plus years in that same TV market. Even though I changed jobs after finishing my certification as a meteorologist and changed stations from the CBS to the NBC affiliate in the market, I stayed planted in the same place for most of my television career.

WINTER DISTRACTIONS

For much of the year, I love the climate in Michigan. From late spring through summer and into late fall, the weather, on average, ranges from beautiful to tolerable.

It's only the unseasonably cold days of spring and fall and bitter wintry days of winter I cannot stand. Getting through that part of the year while my nest was full was much more manageable. As a parent of three busy athletes, there was always a lot to do and many activities that provided great distractions. All three of my kids played hockey, which was an absolute blast to watch! And my youngest filled our winter months with basketball!

LONG, COLD WINTER

It's only now that all of it is over, that living in the northern climate seems almost unbearable.

When the icy winds blow, and it's impossible to get outside to do any of the activities I love, like walking, biking, and playing golf, I regret the decision not to plant myself some place warmer.

GETTING A SOUTHERN NEST

Does the Empty Nest season feel to you like a long, cold winter? A seasonal climate change may be what you need to help break the ice.

Of all fifty states, I have fallen in love with the State of Florida. Besides the promise of the "sunshine state" filling my life with bright and warm weather year-round, my sweet baby grandson lives in Tampa. Perhaps there is another locale for you to visit, too. Try to see someplace with a different climate and a different pace of life. If your grandkids live nearby, then all the better.

 ## LIVING A FULL LIFE

- As you're getting older, what are your feelings about the climate where you spend most of your time?
- Is there a way for you to spend time in another climate? How can you work to make this happen?
- What are the emotions you feel as you ponder starting another chapter of your life in a brand-new place?

SELF-IMPROVEMENT TIME

——

*Only put off until tomorrow what you are willing
to die having left undone.*

Pablo Picasso

Chapter 19
From Bugs To Broadcasting

———•———

The biggest adventure you can ever take
is to live the life of your dreams.

Oprah Winfrey

I used to have a spirit of adventure. The journey toward getting my initial bachelor's degree from college was filled with lots of twists and turns. I attended four different colleges in three states, changing my major a handful of times along the way. Add the two schools in two more states that it took for me to complete my Meteorology training, and my collection of college transcripts looks like a travelogue outline. The constant state of change in my life, even though I was moving toward the eventual goal of a college degree, was driven by uncertainty. I knew I wanted a career I would find fulfilling and challenging, but I could not commit to a specific track. From declaring a major in business, then switching to accounting, and eventually hotel/restaurant administration, I was getting nearly straight As in a series of classes that left me *bored*.

As I contemplated the beginning of my junior year of college, I concluded the only logical next step in my journey would be to drop out of college. I went from being the student who was on the Dean's List every single semester to college dropout. After breaking the news to my surprised (and disappointed) parents, I moved back home and began to search for myself. My job search landed me a spot on the team at Orkin Exterminating as a sales/customer service associate. The job title was significantly more glamorous than my daily tasks. For eight-hours a day, I sat in an office that smelled like chemicals and tried my best to "name that bug" based on an over-the-phone description from the caller. Let me know if you ever want an explanation of the difference between carpenter ants and termites. It's quite fascinating.

While the Orkin Exterminating job was not my dream job, it was an essential stop on my journey. One day, a visitor to the office would point me down the path to a new opportunity in the world of media. This young lady stopped in to sell the owner some advertising on my favorite radio station. Commercial radio (and TV) provides programming, entertainment, and news, either free or for a minimal charge to the listener or viewer by selling advertising. Businesses purchase those commercials (spots, as we call them) to promote their products or services to potential customers. The advertiser pays for the airtime and creates a message designed to connect with consumers, hoping to get their business.

I crossed paths with that same young woman just a few weeks later. I introduced myself and asked about the qualifications needed to pursue a position like hers. She told me her station was looking to hire an additional sales rep and gave me the information to reach her boss. They hired me for the job and I traded my adventures in pest control for the world of radio sales.

During this time working in sales, I had the chance to meet and become friends with some young reporters and anchors working on my hometown television stations. To me, it looked as though the people who were ON THE AIR had fun and meaningful jobs. So, after a few short months, I knew I was ready for yet another change in my life.

I returned to college to pursue a degree in Communications and Broadcast Journalism. From the first class, I felt an excitement that had been missing in any other course I had taken. I discovered excellent opportunities to volunteer for on-air positions at the campus radio station, especially during the very early morning hours. I threw myself into my studies and volunteered at the campus radio and television stations. At the beginning of the summer before my senior year, I was ready for an internship. I again moved back to my hometown, this time as an intern at the television station which had inspired me to pursue my current path. I was excited and ready for a great adventure.

The summer internship began with me 'learning the ropes. I made the rounds to the police and sheriff's department with the veteran reporters. I learned how to sift through reports and bookings at the jail. I listened to scanners, made beat calls, learned how to shoot and edit with the station's equipment. I wrote scripts and eventually had a few of my stories make the air! Just a few weeks into the internship and I was getting and earning lots of great opportunities. My most significant break came when the weekend anchor got a new job and moved to a bigger market. Since my hometown is one of the smallest television markets in the country, the News Director asked ME if I would fill in for the next several weeks while he was searching for a replacement.

My response: Absolutely, positively, 100 percent yes!

Eventually, I was offered a job in a much bigger market, Green Bay. The university I was attending was in the Green Bay market, so by accepting the CBS affiliate position in Green Bay, I could also finish the rest of the classes I needed to earn my Bachelor of Science degree.

When I look back on that time in my life, it seems like different person's life journey.

Over the past few decades, giving my children a full life in a full nest meant creating stability. I went from a person of adventure to a creature of habit. Now that they are building their nests, it's time to go back to the future and start creating my new adventures. I am digging deep to reconnect with the old Terri to see if I can incorporate any of the wonderfully free-spirited, adventurous, and creative parts of her life into the Terri of today.

When you become an empty nester, you enter a season in which you'll have more control over your life. What you want to do and when you want to do it takes priority over everything you have to do for everyone else.

While at first you may battle feelings of being unessential or unimportant, this season also comes with the opportunity to accomplish all those things you put on hold.

The Empty Nest season is when we get to reestablish our identities as individuals. We can enter the workforce or learn new job skills, change careers, take on a new hobby or develop a new skill. We can even go back to school as a student or teacher. Our options are as open to us now as they were in our Growing Up season and Young Adult season.

My challenge to you (and myself) is to figure out who you were before you were mom and who you want to be *now* and *next*.

LIVING A FULL LIFE

- Who were you before you were mom?
- When you look back at the turning points in your life, were the events that produced changes in your life ones you pursued, or those that happened to you?
- What are your personality characteristics that may have been buried during the Juggling Act season? How can you connect with those you deeply miss during the Empty Nest season?

Chapter 20
Get Ready For Your Adventures

———•———

Think for a minute, darling: in fairy tales it's always the children who have the fine adventures. The mothers have to stay at home and wait for the children to fly in the window.
Audrey Niffenegger, *The Time Traveler's Wife*

I had to chuckle when I found the above quote from *The Time Traveler's Wife*.

It made me think of when my kids had social plans, especially on a Friday or Saturday night. My biggest adventure (after figuring out what I was going to watch on TV to entertain myself while they were gone) was trying to stay awake, so I could hear about their night when they got home.

Even those social experiences for our kids came in waves of transition. The elementary and middle school years may involve a trip to the movies, skating, or bowling. With kids that age, parents would be the chauffeur for the evening. I would drive at least part of the carpool. I always viewed driving the carpool as one of my week's highlights since I would get to experience my kids' energy, enthusiasm, and sometimes their friends as they were heading out to spend a few social hours without the adults tagging along.

As the kids transitioned into high school and earned their driver's licenses, the carpool part of the night was no longer something that required my help. My kids and their friends could come and go on their own. My only opportunity to experience the enthusiasm, excitement, and energy surrounding the evening's plans was when they were leaving and when they would come home. I would try to stay awake so I could hear a little about the adventure, but with my early work schedule, I was not always successful at staying awake until they came home. Even if I stayed awake, it wasn't a guarantee they would take the time to have a chat about their night.

When I was in high school, I remember several occasions when I was having a lot of fun, wondering if my parents were bored, just sitting at home by themselves watching television.

As my kids were growing up in our active nest, those nights when they were out with friends often gave me peace and quiet (and access to the remote control) that were quite rare.

Now that the nest is empty, almost every evening involves quiet time and lack of excitement. The Empy Nest stage provides us with the opportunity to plan activities of our own.

The adventure or activity can be long, short, active, low-key, solo, or with a group of friends.

MY IDEAS:
- Go to a matinee movie in the middle of the afternoon.
- Join a bowling league.

- Join (or start) a book club.
- Plan to meet up with friends for a happy hour.
- Go to a museum, the library, or a concert.
- Attend a lecture or educational program.
- If you are financially able, plan a getaway with friends.

I recently went away on a "girls golf weekend" with five other women from my golf course community. We are of different ages and in different life stages, but the common thread connecting us was our desire to have a mid-winter golf getaway to a warm destination. The inaugural adventure timing was mid-February, so we called it the "GAL-entines Golf Weekend." In the Juggling Act seasons, I would have been reluctant to spend the time, money, or energy to get away with a group of women. In the Empty Nest season, I discovered the energy and rejuvenation that lead me to look for other opportunities to connect with women in planning adventures. (Planning for the 2nd Annual GAL-entines Golf Weekend is already underway.)

What's important is to make a plan. Part of an adventure is the anticipation and looking forward to having something special to do.

Often, the curse of an empty nest is we no longer have full calendars. Not only are we often unneeded for daily activities, we can go for days or weeks and feel as though we have nothing worthwhile to do! Instead of considering this as a time of being unnecessary, try shifting the way you think about the calendar's emptiness. Look at this as a time of *freedom* to engage in activities that boost our energy and spirit.

Planning even a small adventure can create an enormous boost in spirits!

LIVING A FULL LIFE

- What adventures did you put off planning when your life revolved around your kids?
- What's stopping you from planning events and activities you enjoy?
- How do you feel when you have something to look forward to?

Chapter 21
Go Back To School

———•———

Education is the key to unlocking the world,
a passport to freedom.

Oprah Winfrey

There's a name in higher education used to describe an older student returning to college or starting college after being away for a number of years or even decades—a "nontraditional."

Nontraditional, but certainly not uncommon.

GRAYING OF COLLEGE CAMPUSES

According to a Forbes article from 2018, adult learners are now the majority of degree seekers on college campuses in the United States.[14] Expanded access to higher education means older students don't even have to live in dorms or fraternity/sorority houses.

Online learning opportunities have exploded in recent years, creating an affordable and accessible way for men and women to return to the classroom, even a virtual classroom, without disrupting their entire lives. During the Coronavirus Pandemic of 2020, many colleges and universities were forced to offer most, or even all, courses online, creating expanded opportunities for distance learning for years to come.

A wide variety of reasons can be the motivation for returning to the classroom, like learning a new skill set or trying to get a leg up in an evolving industry. But sometimes the joy of learning can be its own motivator!

The Forbes article outlines four key reasons people over the age of fifty decide to return to the classroom as a student:

1. PREPARING FOR A SECOND CAREER

After spending an entire career in the workforce, earning a living, and raising a family, there are often passions and interests an empty nester can develop and use in a second act career. This could be the time to pursue a more meaningful path; perhaps something in social services or education. Organizations in the nonprofit world are always looking for experienced leadership. Sometimes, a shift in a career strategy can require going back to school.

2. STAYING COMPETITIVE IN THE WORKFORCE

This is especially the case in technology-focused fields, where quickly evolving systems, like computer hardware or software, can easily create a circumstance where an older adult can find themselves passed over for opportunities or promotions in favor of a younger person who is keeping up with the changes and expertise.

Going back to school, even taking a few classes regularly, can allow an older person to stay more competitive in their current field.

3. CREATING NEW CHALLENGES AND LEARNING NEW THINGS

Have you always wanted to learn a language? Or get more technologically proficient? Get that advanced certification? There are lots of degreed and non-degree opportunities available in the twenty-first century. Online classes make it possible to easily connect to programs in just about every field of study, often offered at low or even free costs.

4. MEETING A LONG-HELD GOAL

This can be the motivator for someone who always wanted to finish or get a degree but got off track somewhere along the way.

COGNITIVE CONNECTIONS

An in-person classroom situation will allow the empty-nester to create new connections with classmates, even becoming part of small study groups. These groups can allow more in-depth exploration of the material covered in the classroom, energetic conversations about the subject, and how it may relate to current events. This opportunity to engage in discussions with new people will help create intellectual and emotional connections. Taking a few classes at either a community college or local university is often a great way to surround yourself with like-minded classmates who will help you find inspiration and excitement while producing a bit of a challenge.

You will have a purpose to get up in the morning and a reason to stay off the couch and turn off the TV in the afternoon and evening. But don't forget about the homework! You'll have to study and write papers!

Getting (or finishing) that degree doesn't even have to be the end goal. Increasing knowledge, finding a challenge, and creating new relationships are great reasons to take the leap and head back to school.

LIVING A FULL LIFE

- What skill or area of knowledge do you find most interesting?
- Even if there is not much of a monetary pay-off, which career have you always wanted to explore? Day Trader? Social Worker? Licensed Counselor? Art Teacher?
- Think back to your Growing-Up season to your dream job? What skills or knowledge would you have to attain to reach that goal?

Chapter 22
Create A Career Encore

---•---

*In the world of business, the people who are most successful
are those who are doing what they love.*

Warren Buffett

Hitting the Empty Nest season and turning fifty means that, for
those in the workforce, they probably have at least ten to twenty
years left in their professional life. For others who spent the
Juggling Act season as a stay-at-home parent, this might be their
first chance to enter the workforce. According to a Pew Research
article from 2018,[15] one in five moms and dads are stay-at-home
parents. More than eleven million parents were not working
outside the home in 2016, almost identical to the statistics from
1989, though in 2016, there was a modest increase in the number
of fathers in this role.

WHAT'S YOUR CAREER SECOND ACT?

Regardless of the work we are doing, we no longer do it just because it was always what we had done or were trained to do.

Now that the nest is empty and the financial demands of life may not be as high, this is an excellent stage to think about how to invest the skills, talents, and expertise we have developed from so many years as a mom and use those to do something else meaningful. The value of being a stay-at-home parent is extraordinarily high. An article[16] on the website Salary.com places the estimated annual salary for a stay-at-home parent's work in 2018 at $162,581. The article outlines that the skill set possessed by that stay-at-home parent ranged from accountant and bookkeeper to nurse, plumber, psychologist, teacher, chef, and more.

Is this the time where we step away from the corporate world and work for a nonprofit?

For someone who has always had a job in one place, is this the time to consider taking a position that will involve more travel?

For someone who has always worked in a big corporate setting, is this the time to move to a smaller organization? Or someone who always has been in a small organization, is this the time to step into corporate America? For stay-at-home moms, is this the time to step into the workforce, using all the skills learned while running the small corporation known as a household?

Or is this the time to look for new opportunities in your current place of employment? I'm blessed to work for a fellow empty nester, Julie Brinks, who looks for hidden or unrealized skills and talents in the people on her team and encourages them to spread their wings. Julie has excellent instincts about the future of our industry, and as a working mom who raised successful sons, she can see the potential for growth. Discovering new opportunities for a career encore in this environment doesn't even require a change of venue!

VOCATIONAL SECOND (OR THIRD) ACT

AARP is an organization for people age fifty and up. According to an AARP report, for a majority of Americans, retirement barely exists anymore.[17] Some older Americans keep working out of financial necessity, but many others work because it keeps them connected and fulfilled.

As people remain more active into their later years, most of us will have more time to spend on a career "re-boot." AARP supports a special program called Encore[18] that helps older adults find meaning and purpose in life. Encore dates back to the late 90s and was developed because of considerable interest from people interested in finding a new position or path in life after stepping away from what had been a decades-long career. Most of those interested in encore careers were looking to work fewer than thirty hours a week.

The Encore Career Handbook, written by Marci Alboher, states that even if an older worker doesn't get paid, they want to remain connected, relevant, useful, and engaged. These are feelings similar to what an empty nester may have felt in that "we're not done yet."[19]

The idea here is to figure out if there is a professional dream you may have always held and not waste time deciding if it's worth pursuing. Associate State Director for AARP Michigan, Jennifer Feuerstein, says "Deciding what you want to do when you 'grow up' can be overwhelming. So really consider what your dream job would be and why. Asking the why is critical. As you explore your encore career path, you may decide you want to phase into retirement, instead of going 'cold turkey'. This could include cutting back hours or taking on a new role with less responsibilities. The best part is that you really get to explore and try new things. And if it doesn't work, you're in the stage of life where you can make changes."

If you have always been an employee, but never a manager, but you have those leadership desires, is this the time to apply for a managerial position?

Or is this the time in life to start your own business? AARP's Feuerstein says entrepreneurs who launch and build a business in the second half of life—over the age of fifty—are one of the fastest growing groups of business owners. Research from the Small Business Administration shows one in four individuals ages forty-four to seventy are interested in becoming entrepreneurs. If you fall into that category and don't know where to start, check out AARP's Work For Yourself@50+ [20] which provides support and information to help you get started.

"Finding your encore career begins with asking "what's my 'what's next?'" Sometimes you know exactly what you what to do. Sometimes the answer isn't so clear. The idea of an encore is saving the best for last. And this is your opportunity to carve out the late-stage career that you really desire," says Feuerstein.

If you think you would like to have more control and hang out your own shingle, it is worth exploring the opportunities presented in today's world.

Are you crafty and would like to create things you can sell on the Internet, perhaps on a site like Etsy?

If you are a real go-getter, there are opportunities in multi-level marketing and networking organizations.

I have always found my greatest energy and joy comes from being needed. Maybe you feel this way too. If that's the case, and you are blessed to have financial flexibility in this season of life, your plan to take the next step in your vocational ladder may allow you to explore options that have a bigger pay-off than just dollar signs. Feuerstein agrees. "The benefit of building an encore career is to have a more financially secure and emotionally enjoyable retirement by working in a job you find meaningful."

 ## LIVING A FULL LIFE

- Have you considered changing your profession during this season or entering the workforce if you are not already working?
- If you have been working, how do you feel about your job? Is it draining or fulfilling? Is there a job or career field that would fill you with excitement and energy?
- Is there a business you have wanted to start? Can you think of a way to "hang out your own shingle" in a field that would fill you with excitement and energy?

Chapter 23
Hobbies
No Longer Driving A Carpool
And Writing Checks

———•———

Find three hobbies you love: One to make you money, one to keep
you in shape, and one to be creative.

Anonymous

While our nests are full, we rarely have the extra time or resources
to explore a creative outlet on our own. Heck, I barely had time
to fold clothes or empty the dishwasher. However, we create a
myriad of opportunities for our children to explore their hobbies,
investing our time, money, and energy.

Transitioning into an empty nest gives us lots of open hours in
our week, and for some of us, it provides extra resources.

It's time to explore some options you may have never considered in the past. For example, I was recently invited to produce a

painting for a benefit art auction. I never thought of myself as having any artistic ability. But the organizers of this event paired me with a wonderful elementary school art teacher, who happened to already to be a friend of mine, Kathleen Broekhuizen. She is also an empty nester and married to my daughter's former high school soccer coach.

It turns out Kathleen is quite a talented coach in the world of watercolor painting. In the style of Bob Ross, she coached me through creating a landscape watercolor. I would never have imagined I would be able to create! Because of this experience, I am looking forward to exploring more art creations.

But striking a chord in my previously undiscovered art gene has led me to dig deep about some other areas of life I would love to learn, or at least *try*!

Here's My Top 10 List:
1. Learn to juggle
2. Learn to play the piano
3. Learn to sew
4. Learn to make fabric bows for gift baskets
5. Learn to solve the Rubik's Cube
6. Explore my newly discovered artistic skills
7. Improve my golf skills
8. Improve my tennis skills
9. Join a bowling league
10. Learn yoga

Try writing your own top ten list. The Empty Nest season allows us the opportunity to pursue some of those hobbies. Make the most of it!

 ## LIVING A FULL LIFE

- Is there an interest or passion you have not pursued because you did not have the time or resources?
- Is there something you remember doing with great passion in the years before you had children? Would you be interested in trying it again today?
- Who do you know who could help you develop your interest or passion?

Chapter 24
How To Enjoy Being Alone

———•———

Loneliness is not a lack of company, loneliness is a lack of purpose.
Guillermo Maldonado

There is a lack of privacy that goes along with the child-raising years.

I have friends with little kids who say they can't even go to the bathroom or take a shower without little hands pounding on the door and yelling, "Mommy, are you in there?"

It seems like those years are filled with "never alone" time. The lack of solitude and privacy can sometimes overwhelm a parent with little ones.

Fast forward to the empty nest, and it seems like there is so much alone time that the silence and solitude can seem overwhelming.

For me, that was one of the hardest adjustments to make when I was emptying the nest.

I craved the company.

I craved companionship.

I craved having someone around, even if we weren't talking.

I just love having someone else around. That's especially the case when that someone is a person I enjoy talking to, listening to, just quietly hanging out.

There is a vast difference in being alone and being lonely. For me, those were the same things at the beginning of my Empty Nest season. I was alone, and I was *lonely*!

Adjusting to the alone time involves finding enjoyable things to do by yourself. Depending on your mood and ambition-level, these activities can be thoughtful, inspirational, or just a mindless way to spend a few hours.

Here are just a few options I discovered:

- Reading fiction (Entertaining)
- Reading non-fiction (Educational, Inspirational)
- Watching Hallmark® movies (there's always a happy ending)
- Taking a walk
- Binge-watching a Netflix® show
- Hopscotch through TED Talks on YouTube®

HOW AN OBSESSION LED TO ACTION

One of my absolute favorite ways to spend countless solo hours is listening to podcasts. Almost by accident, I discovered this treasure-trove of free programs on my iPhone. Many of these programs are interesting and informative. I have gained inspiration and enthusiasm for taking on new projects by listening to people interested in the same things.

I may have never taken a leap of faith and wrote this book without discovering other authors and publishers with their own podcast. My newfound obsession turned into *action* for my Empty Nest season.

And, unlike many other things, listening to a podcast is often a solo activity. I put on my headphones, grab my iPhone, call up the latest episode and start taking a walk. I felt less lonely while listening to great podcasts. The voices of authentic people on the other side of my earbuds lit a fire in me to do my creative work. I liked what I heard so much I started my own podcast.

Maybe one day, you will look for a way to fill your quiet time, and you'll stumble upon my familiar voice. Regardless, look for podcasts, videos, and books that can help you in a similar way the voices of those strangers in podcast land helped me. Enjoy being alone by finding inspiration in new places.

 LIVING A FULL LIFE

- How do you spend your alone hours right now?
- Is there an activity you want to try—a personal goal or a hobby—best experienced by a party of one?
- Try searching YouTube®, a podcast app, or your local library's online catalog for information about one of the hobbies you listed in the previous chapter. Look for something that inspires you to dig deeper into that subject.

Chapter 25
My Husband Says My Tombstone Will Say, "I Was Gonna"

———•———

The moment you have an instinct to act on a goal, you must physically move within five seconds or your brain will stop you. 5-4-3-2-1-GO!

Mel Robbins

My husband always jokes that my tombstone is going to read, "I was gonna."

I've always been one of those people who take a long time to get started at something, but once I get going, I'm a hard person to stop. A big part of the reason is that I fully understand the energy I will dedicate to something once I decide it is a worthwhile task.

This is the case for so many things in my life, from getting out of bed on a random slow Saturday morning to folding the laundry, cooking dinner, or tackling a personal goal.

MEL ROBBINS

I stumbled across a TED Talk video given by an inspirational woman who incidentally has gone on to get her own talk show! Her thesis applied to me as it was about getting started. By now, you may have heard of Mel Robbins, but I'm proud to say I had heard of her before the launch of her talk show, as I must have watched her TED Talk at least thirty or forty times.

In this twenty-one minute and forty-second talk, which she called How to Stop Screwing Yourself Over, she outlined the simple strategy for getting everything we want in life. [21]

Simple, but not easy.

The part of her strategy that resonated with me was the importance of just getting started . . . with everything.

- Getting out of bed in the morning.
- Doing something tough.
- Doing something time consuming.
- Getting into shape.

Her recipe for success? Toward the end of her talk, she gave the secret ingredient!

She started counting backward, "5-4-3-2-1-GO!"

When you get to the end of the countdown, move.

No hitting the snooze alarm.

No more excuses.

You just move and get started.

Of course, her talk also tackled the importance of understanding the reasons we don't get started. She said most people are waiting to feel like they want to do something. But guess what? We rarely feel like we want to do anything to get started. Even though we may like how something feels when we are in the middle of it, completing it, or even starting it, the act of getting started is the most crucial part.

So, for me, that triggered action! In an absolute leap of faith, I decided to send an email to invite a person I met at a book launch a few years earlier to meet for coffee and discuss the concept I had for this book.

Just like that!

I counted backward . . . 5-4-3-2-1-GO . . . hit the SEND key and waited.

At that moment, I had the same feeling I always get when I decide to jump into a pool. As I am in the air over the water, I know I will land in the water, but not how it will feel. Or how I am going to feel. But once you take off and are in the air, it is too late to turn back. I suppose there might be a way to un-send an email, but I don't have that part of technology figured out. That's probably a good thing.

Because that leap of faith did not end with me soaking wet in a swimming pool, it ended with me writing these words you are reading right now.

And speaking of writing, my husband is going to have to re-work the caption on my tombstone.

At least for this dream of mine, it will have to read, "She said she was gonna . . . and she did!"

 LIVING A FULL LIFE

- Are you a procrastinator about everything or just big things?
- What have you been putting off?
- What could you accomplish if you tried a strategy of counting down 5-4-3-2-1?

FORECASTING
A HEALTHIER YOU

Our bodies are our gardens. Our wills are our gardeners.

William Shakespeare

Chapter 26
Fifty Is The New Thirty

———•———

Beautiful young people are accidents of nature,
but beautiful old people are works of art.
Eleanor Roosevelt

Becoming an empty nester coincides with the shift into mid-life as we age into our forties and fifties. Turning fifty is a significant milestone. If we are fortunate enough to live to be one hundred years old, fifty is the midpoint. Since we won't all live to be one hundred, fifty is actually past the midpoint. As I turned fifty, my mortality became clear. I was closer to the end of my life than the beginning.

Even though that might be a reality for nearly everyone, turning fifty doesn't have to mean we are on the fast track to old age.

It's easier to take better care of ourselves than ever before. We have greater access to vitamins, nutrients, and we can make time to cultivate healthier living habits. Because of this, there is a phrase kicked around pretty commonly when people turn fifty: fifty is the new thirty!

ACHES AND PAINS OF THE SEASON

Yet even though the Empty Nest season allows us to focus on healthier living, for many of us, it is also the season when we feel aches and pains doing things that never used to bother us. I'll confess, when I get up in the morning and take my first steps, the bottoms of my feet often ache. I may have a difficult time standing straight up. As time goes on, all those feelings of discomfort become more pronounced.

TIME TO GET STARTED

As we think about forecasting a healthier life stage, it is essential we value our physical bodies. This means eating right, regular exercise and movement, drinking enough water, and getting enough sleep. As we were raising our kids, especially those of us who had kids who were athletes, we watched our kids go to training and competition, always pushing themselves to get stronger, faster, and staying as healthy as possible. If your story is anything like mine, I had plenty of opportunities for my kids to be in better physical shape, but for me, that was not always a priority. I would sacrifice sleep on a regular basis.

Now, all that needs to change! Today is the best shape we are ever going to be in unless we do something about it. While we cannot turn back the hands of time, we can get started. Getting started can be as easy as taking a walk, planning healthier meals, and going to bed earlier, so we are not depriving our bodies of the essential sleep we need.

WHAT THE CORONAVIRUS TAUGHT US

As if this wasn't a commonsense approach, we all know we should take, the Coronavirus Pandemic of 2020 was a clear wake-up call for many of us. The people who were the most vulnerable to having the harshest effects from the virus were those individuals who were already suffering from significant physical issues. Those who were overweight, especially if they are also diagnosed with heart disease and diabetes, were most vulnerable. In general, the healthiest people were the most likely to fight off the disease with short-term symptoms that allowed them to recover fully.

The coronavirus is just one recent example of why we need to take better care of ourselves and get healthier. Indeed, forecasting a healthier you will mean valuing your health and being willing to take the steps and lifestyle changes to turn the corner toward healthier and fuller living.

 LIVING A FULL LIFE

- Do you value your health? If your answer is yes, how do you show it to yourself?
- Name one exercise you can add to your daily routine, even if it's just stretching to start.
- What did you learn about health (and creating a healthier you) during the Coronavirus Pandemic of 2020?

Chapter 21
Cereal And $5 Pizzas . . .
Eat Better

———◆———

Sorry, there's no magic bullet. You gotta eat healthy and live
healthy to be healthy and look healthy. End of story.
Morgan Spurlock

One day, my son Jacob came home from spending an afternoon
with his wife Taylor's family and asked me, "Hey, just curious,
what did we eat when we were growing up? I don't remember ever
eating, I know we must've eaten, but I just don't remember it."

Of course, the reporter in me needed to ask a follow-up question so I could get a little perspective as to where this question was
coming from, so I said, "Why are you asking?"

"We were sitting around at Taylor's house after dinner and
talking about our favorite foods, and I said; honestly, I don't remember eating much of anything. I mean, I know we ate, but I
just don't remember it!"

"What about cereal? Remember eating cereal?" I asked. "How about the five-dollar pizzas from Little Caesars? Does that ring a bell with you?"

We had a great laugh, and I realized that even though nutrition and mealtime was an important part of the family dynamics, I had fallen short on that front.

I'll be the first one to admit I was often terrible at planning and executing meals for our family when our children were growing up. My excuse is we were always running from one sporting activity to another, often shuttling our multiple kids to multiple different activities, hopscotching from one location to another in a single night. As a result, mealtime was often a matter of eating what we could grab and chow down in the car. I am sorry to say we didn't always have the most nutritious foods available for the "grab and go" dining options for three very athletic kids. On the afternoons when the kids would be happy to grab Subway®, I felt like we were knocking it out of the park in terms of healthy food.

It has been interesting for me to watch my kids and their spouses take a huge interest in cooking. They experiment with recipes and flavors and eat healthy ingredients. They would rather cook their food and eat at home than go out for a meal (unless it's a very nice restaurant and my husband and I happen to be paying).

I'm taking a lesson from this: to live as healthy as possible, I need to take a more dedicated interest in preparing food and eating a more nutritious diet. Not necessarily because of the interest in losing weight, but because I recognize food is a vital part of a healthy lifestyle. Living healthy requires putting good fuel in my body. The best vitamins and nutrients come from the food we eat, as our bodies are processing them.

Yes, I am embarrassed cereal and five-dollar pizza dinners were the culinary cornerstones of my parenting years, but I am now trying to do better. My empty nest has a full pantry of healthy ingredients.

LIVING A FULL LIFE

- Do you look back at mealtimes with your children with fondness or melancholy?
- How have mealtimes changed for you now that you are living in an empty nest?
- How has the way you think about food changed, now that you no longer have the demands of children or a busy schedule? What can you do to make sure these changes are healthy?

Chapter 28
Get Moving—The Year
I Ran Nine 5ks

•

Running is the greatest metaphor for life
because you get out of it what you put into it.
Oprah Winfrey

I've gone through streaks of exercise in my life. I've never really been a runner, but I did train for a 5k for the first time when my youngest was in middle school. The effort was to prepare for our school's version of a Girls on the Run program.[22] I made it through the training because I had a buddy who was about the same couch-potato level as I was at the time. It was ironic because her daughter ended up running cross-country, and my daughter was a successful all-around athlete at the same age.

We moms were happy just driving the girls to where they need to be, grabbing a cappuccino from the gas station, and then sitting at practice chatting while we watched the girls go through their training. As I look back on that time, I think it would've been a great time to have just grabbed a bottle of water, our walking shoes and spent the hour or so while the girls were at practice getting in a bit of physical activity. But of course, when we were younger, in our thirties and forties, it didn't seem like we were motivated to put in the effort. Plus, it was easy to find excuses because of the exhausting schedule we kept.

GOAL ACCOMPLISHED

I was so proud of us when we finished the 5k. My goal at the time was to not walk. The girls went at their own pace. My daughter Jenn passed me on the course. She was finishing her second mile as I was finishing my first. She was booking it! After she finished the race, she ran the last mile with me, probably logging five miles herself that day.

That was the only 5k I ran that year. Looking back on that time, I wish I would've stayed engaged with running or jogging. Doing the physical work to get to the point where I could do the 5k, even though I wasn't breaking any land speed records, was the hard part. If I would've just dedicated myself to running a mile and a half three times a week, I could have kept myself in better shape.

Fast forward to the year my youngest was graduating from high school. It was a pivotal year, as she was moving away to college and leaving the nest so much emptier. I became close through AAU basketball with one of the moms on her team, whose daughter was Jenn's roommate. Her nest was emptying at the same time as mine. She is a few years younger than me and also more dedicated to fitness than I was. We made a pact that year that we would sign up and run several 5k events. There are multiple reasons this was a great strategy.

First, most of these happen on Saturday mornings, which were hard mornings for the newly empty nesters. When our girls were living at home and in school, Saturday mornings were busy with school sports or AAU, so to suddenly not have any obligations made it a very painful time of the week for us.

There is also such a social aspect of running in a 5k due to race events' camaraderie. Besides the physical fitness benefits of running, there is a physical rush of endorphins from working out. A sense of community comes from being surrounded by people looking to connect and engage with people trying to take better care of themselves.

That year I ran nine 5ks!

The next couple of years, I only ran a couple 5ks and switched my active time from running to biking.

Now I have settled on walking as my favorite activity. I have a personal goal of walking at least 10,000 steps every day. I keep track using a Fitbit since my personality's competitive side is motivated by setting and hitting my personal daily goal. Much of the time, I put my iPhone in my fanny pack and listen to a favorite podcast on a solo adventure. Still, I will occasionally meet up with a friend or invite my husband along for the journey. During the cold and snow season in West Michigan, a local shopping mall replaces sidewalks and nature trails for my adventure route. Mall walking is a great activity for the Empty Nest season, though it's a good idea to leave the credit cards at home!

The bottom line, being physically active is crucial in this stage of our life. It is critical to keep our bodies moving, maintain muscle tone, and keep tone. It's also essential for bone health and our mental health benefits, especially when we are outside doing activities.

This is the best shape I am ever going to be in my life. I don't have time to waste; daily activity is an essential part of thriving in an empty nest.

LIVING A FULL LIFE

- How have you prioritized getting physical exercise regularly?
- Is there someone you regularly could meet to have activities with you?
- What is holding you back from exercise and daily intentional physical activities?

Chapter 29
Sleep Is Not Over-Rated

———•———

Sleep is the golden chain that ties health and our bodies together.
Thomas Dekker

I had an overly used saying when the kids were young and active, while I was burning the candle at both ends. Daily, I used to say, "Sleep is overrated." This favorite saying grew from the fact I would go through stretches where I would only get four or perhaps five hours of sleep per night. A big part of that was because the beginning part of my day started so early. As a morning meteorologist of a television show that begins at 4:30 a.m., the alarm clock for me rings no later than 2:45 a.m., regardless of when I went to bed the night before.

Because of the super early wake-up call every morning, a bedtime of 9:45 p.m. would get me only five hours of shut-eye. To get that magical eight hours of sleep, I would have to be in bed and asleep by 6:45 p.m. There were so many nights my kids' activities didn't even start until 7:00 or 7:30 p.m.

So, I was shortchanging my sleep for many years.

I didn't realize how much it affected me, and how I got through life feeling like I was in a perpetual state of jet lag. I seldom felt completely refreshed. Even on the weekends, there were few opportunities for sleeping in. It was a matter of shuttling kids to multiple events, tournaments, games, training, or practices. Whatever the case, even the weekends would include significantly less than the recommended eight hours.

So, how important is it to get a good night's sleep? What is that magic number? Do we need more sleep as we get older? These are terrific questions research is examining. According to an article in *Medical News Today*, getting enough sleep is vital in the following areas of life:

- Better productivity and concentration
- Lower weight gain risk
- Better calorie regulation
- Greater athletic performance
- Lower risk of heart disease
- More social and emotional intelligence
- Preventing depression
- Lower inflammation
- Stronger immune systems[23]

So, how much sleep do we need? According to the National Sleep Foundation, the average adult requires between seven and nine hours per night.[24]

As an empty nester, the key for me is to get to bed at a much more reasonable time since I still work that early morning shift.

With nobody to drive around and no evening activities to watch, I have no excuses for not getting to bed by at least 7:00 in the evening.

This is the time to commit yourself. It starts with adjusting your daily schedule, so you finish activities and try to wind down by a decent time each night. For me, that is around six o'clock in the evening. Getting to bed earlier is a crucial commitment I have made for this next stage in my life.

As members of the Empty Nest Club, many excuses for putting off our health have fallen by the wayside. We have only ourselves to blame when we don't take care of our health, and a key part of that includes getting enough sleep.

 LIVING A FULL LIFE

- How much sleep do you get on an average night?
- Do you consider sleep to be an essential part of staying healthy?
- Are there changes you can make in your regular schedule that will allow you to get at least eight hours of sleep per night?

NATURAL RESOURCES

———

As you grow older, you will discover that you have two hands:
one for helping yourself, the other for helping others.

Audrey Hepburn

Chapter 30

We make a living by what we get, but we
make a life by what we give.
Winston Churchill

Raising a child is not just an emotional investment. It costs *a lot* of money.

According to federal government statistics, it costs more than a quarter of a million dollars to raise a child from birth to age eighteen.[25]

Just think about that! $284,570 . . . and that's just for the basics!

It doesn't include private school tuition or a car or travel basketball or piano lessons.

Our kids' growing-up years can stretch our budget. As your kids leave the nest, your financial resources might be more plentiful. It is ironic that as we get to later stages in our careers, we need much less to live on when making more money. And, as our kids leave the nest and become independent adults, they rely on our support a lot less.

So, now that your child has left the nest, do you suddenly feel flush with extra cash? Is there empty room in the budget? If that's the case for you, perhaps now you can start spending some of your resources on things other than child-rearing.

As my nest has emptied, my husband and I are still at least a decade away from retirement. That means there is room in the budget for more discretionary spending. But even though I can spend more money on myself, I continue to spend money on and give money to my adult children, who are now living through the most expensive time in their adult lives. They are just in the beginning stage of their careers; going to graduate school, buying homes, and starting families. Take a few minutes and think about the needs of your adult children. What expenses are they facing? Are there ways you could help?

YOU CAN'T TAKE IT WITH YOU

A couple years ago, I adopted this phrase to describe my philosophy on spending extra cash on my adult children.

I figure, when my husband and I are both gone, they will get it all anyway, so why not get the joy and pleasure in seeing the happiness they express when you splurge for groceries or continue to pay for cell phones or even treat for manicures and pedicures?

My adult kids appreciate these indulgences (some big and some small), but I will admit I selfishly get a reward in return. I love the feeling of knowing I have been a blessing to my adult kids. During the Juggling Act season, buying a particular pair of jeans or athletic shoes can seem like a parent's obligation. During the Empty Nest season, those same purchases are not expected or required; they are optional. Gifts don't have to be reserved for birthdays or Christmas. I get an incredible feeling of excitement buying a special book or clothing item and making a care package to send to my out-of-state kids.

You may also discover the joy of planning and executing a special delivery. Perhaps include a couple gift cards and a box of your child's favorite candy. The immediate reward might be a boost to your spirits when you find you are missing them the most. You might also get a phone call (or text) when that package is received.

BEING GENEROUS TO OTHERS

Have you heard of those stories on the news where a small restaurant server gets an unexpected big tip? Or perhaps it's the social media post about people at a drive-through coffee shop who decide to pay for the person in the car behind them in line. Being generous to someone you may not know can be a great way to impact another person's life in a positive way. This is a way to boost your spirits. Even a small amount can be a big deal to someone who is not expecting it.

MAKING (OR BUYING) MEALS

There can be something incredibly heart-warming to making (or taking) a meal to an individual or family going through a life event. Even on a limited household budget (of time and money) due to graduate school, my daughter Jacqueline and her husband Ben frequently make meals to deliver to friends, fellow church members, or neighbors who are experiencing the birth of a new baby, the death of a loved one, or other medical issues. Their willingness to share their limited resources as a way to bless others is an inspiration to me. The empty nest kitchen can be an excellent place for this type of generosity, with the bonus of connecting to a person or family who will appreciate not having to prepare a meal.

DONATING TO CAUSES AND ORGANIZATIONS

With extra money in the budget, this is also a great time to consider making financial donations to causes and organizations you support. Perhaps you are spending more time volunteering. This could be the time you can make financial contributions to those organizations as well. As you plan your estate, explore making a gift that will become a part of your legacy, perhaps to a school or community organization, to make a difference for future generations. Likely, our contribution won't be enough to get a building named after us. Still, a posthumous gift to a library, church, school, or non-profit organization that can help support a cause you are passionate about now, will be a blessing for those who follow.

 ## LIVING A FULL LIFE

- How has the money you spend on children changed after they left the nest?
- What are the ways you can be generous to people around you, even strangers, or specific causes and organizations now that you are no longer responsible for supporting your children?
- How can you be generous to *yourself* during the Empty Nest season?

Chapter 31
Extra Free Time

———•———

Researchers have settled on what they believe is the magic number
for true expertise: ten thousand hours.

Malcolm Gladwell

One of my favorite authors is Malcolm Gladwell. In his book
Outliers: The Story of Success, Gladwell conducted an extensive
research project to discover how people gain expertise in different
areas. From the way the Beatles became one of the best musical
groups of all time, to the considerable impact Bill Gates and
Steve Jobs made on the computer industry, to even an analysis
of successful attorneys in New York City and some of the most
significant sports icons of all time; the research Gladwell conducted
for this book boiled down to a simple concept; the importance of
a significant investment of time. To become an expert in an area,
a person had to devote a minimum of ten thousand hours to gain
expertise. By the way, to reach ten thousand hours, a person would

have to devote forty hours a week for nearly five years or twenty hours a week for ten years. The book was an in-depth examination of the time invested in developing a mastery in a specific area and exploring how these certain individuals could gain access to the equipment and training it would take to get that magical ten-thousand-hour mark.[26]

As I consider myself an expert in being a parent, I was curious about how much time I had invested in raising each child. When you take the number of hours of sleep away from the equation (eight hours per night), the typical parent has spent sixteen hours per day, three hundred and sixty-five days per year, for eighteen years, to raise their child from birth to adulthood. The calculation is quite incredible! Using that timeline, the average parent has spent over one hundred thousand hours raising each child! So, it is no wonder most parents feel like the investment in that child's life has been extraordinary and a significant level of expertise has been derived from spending all those hours in the parenthood trenches. A parent entering the Empty Nest season could be described as an outlier times ten!

Of course, the only way an outlier could stay focused and energetic enough to invest at least ten thousand hours to gain expertise in an area would be if that person possessed a passion and extreme interest in expertise. With that much passion, could you imagine the difficulty of a Steve Jobs, Bill Gates, or the Beatles stepping away from their area of influence, without some level of discomfort, sadness, or grief?

So, with the typical parent spending at least ten times that many hours raising a child, it is no wonder transitioning into the Empty Nest season is so difficult. Raising a successful child to adulthood is a labor of love involving blood, sweat, tears, and passion.

So, the question for us becomes, should we view the transition to the Empty Nest season as a retirement from that vocation, or is it merely the transition into a new stage in life and relationships? If some level of loss and mourning is expected, how do we process that loss and mourning in a healthy way?

Either way, we know the change will require an investment of time to master. By Gladwell's calculations, it will take you five years before you are a master empty nester. It may not take you long to feel better in this season than you do now. Regardless, give yourself time.

LIVING A FULL LIFE

- Consider how many hours you have invested in raising your child from infancy to adulthood. How does this make you feel?
- In what other areas in your life have you invested at least 10,000 hours?
- With more freedom in your schedule, is there something you want to make a ten-thousand-hour investment in to develop a level of expertise?

Chapter 32
Volunteer

---•---

Life's most persistent and urgent question is,
what are you doing for others?
Dr. Martin Luther King, Jr.

There is a common phrase associated with doing something for someone else, "You get more out of it than you ever put in." This is the case in any volunteer effort, especially during the Empty Nest season.

FIGHTING BOREDOM

A blank calendar can seem more daunting than the jam-packed days and over-scheduled chaos, which was the Juggling Act season's cornerstone. The gaping holes in the daily to-do list can almost trigger a return to the familiar lament of "I'm bored," which is often played on a repeat cycle by kids and teens. "What is there to do?"

BOOSTING PHYSICAL AND MENTAL HEALTH

For empty nesters, the benefits of volunteering include reducing stress, improving mood, and preventing loneliness. A volunteer experience can help an empty nester create new social connections. As I shared earlier, it was through volunteering that I found an enduring friendship with a dear friend, Christy. Volunteering also helps reduce the risk of developing physical ailments like high blood pressure by keeping participants more active and engaged.

HELP WANTED

One of the most significant issues empty nesters face is feeling like they have nothing to contribute or that nobody needs me. In reality, every community has hundreds of organizations that rely on volunteer help. Those special skills developed and honed through decades of parenthood could be put to great use in a hospital or school.

Wondering how to get connected? Do a Google® search of volunteer opportunities in your community, specifying any areas you are interested in helping.

- Love animals? Contact the animal shelter.
- Love to read? Contact a school or library.
- Love babies or small children? Contact a hospital or childcare center.
- Love nature and the outdoors? Contact your county parks department.
- Want to fill the nest? Consider becoming a foster parent.

You've been giving your best to your children. Now is an opportunity to share your best with others. You have so much to give your community. Volunteering can bring a sense of purpose and fulfillment and help create new relationships simultaneously.

 LIVING A FULL LIFE

- What interests in life do you have that could be paired with a volunteer opportunity?
- Do you have a unique passion or area of expertise that could help society?
- If you could do something meaningful, even if you didn't get paid, what would it be?

Chapter 33
Taking Others Under Your Wing

———●———

The delicate balance of mentoring someone is not
creating them in your own image but giving them
the opportunity to create themselves.

Steven Spielberg

As a professional woman in a high-profile position and in an industry previously male-dominated, I often get requests from people involved in mentorship programs. These groups match someone who is an established professional with someone who is just entering that vocation.

Often, the request is for an hour once a week or every other week to counsel and advise a young woman in my profession. The time can be spent helping them solve issues and search for alternative ways of tackling challenges in either starting or advancing a particular career.

While I have not officially signed up to be a part of a structured program, I have often found myself in the role of mentor informally.

As one of the oldest employees at my television station, and the most senior on-air in my role, I take young staff members under my wing to offer guidance, advice, or sometimes just a shoulder to cry on. I have given ideas for contract negotiations and strategies for those seeking advancements. I have encouraged these younger members of our staff to go back to school or even take jobs in smaller markets for the opportunity of making a transition in their careers. These relationships have evolved organically, as we have become coworkers and friends. My role as a trusted advisor is one I earned, as I gained respect as these younger co-workers have worked side-by-side with me.

A mentorship role in a business environment is a little like a parenting role of an adult child. Without being patronizing, you know these young adults are competent and achieving professional success independently. However, you still feel honored they have turned to you for advice, so you can share wisdom to help guide them through some decisions they are making about their future.

Sometimes, someone you have mentored can turn into a valued friend and trusted advisor. She may become a shining star and nationwide household name while reaching professional and personal success by breaking barriers and starting meaningful conversations. Ginger Zee is one of those people in my life.

The world has fallen in love with Ginger Zee as the first female Chief Meteorologist at a major television network, ABC, and the morning face of weather on Good Morning America. On her way to the pinnacle in the world of television weather, Ginger worked alongside me at WOOD-TV. Since she is a "hometown girl" growing up in West Michigan (watching ME on TV), we bonded quickly. Even though I was one of our weather team's senior members, I knew it would be Ginger who would take the world of television and weather by storm. She is a brilliant and energetic young woman who was always the first to volunteer for an extra shift, challenging assignment, or adventure. I was blessed to mentor Ginger for a season of her career and admire her willingness to work hard and dream big.

In addition to her work on television, Ginger has become a best-selling author with her candid memoir *Natural Disaster; I Cover Them I Am One*. In her book, she shares her journey through mental health issues, substance abuse, and an abusive relationship. Ginger's willingness to open her life's struggles to the world has inspired countless people to seek help for their challenges. Ginger has also written an adventurous series of weather-themed fiction books for girls, *Chasing Helicity*, encouraging the next generation of female meteorologists.

After moving on from her work at WOOD-TV to take a job at a television station in Chicago, Ginger became an adjunct professor at Valparaiso University (her alma mater). There she taught a presentation course to future broadcast meteorologists. Ginger became a teacher and mentor to one of my current teammates, Ellen Bacca, in a true act of paying it forward. Ellen then took that adjunct professor spot and is now teaching the class and serving as a mentor herself.

"Traffic Tom (Hillen)" is another colleague who has gone from intern to anchor at our television station. When he joined our morning newscast team as the traffic anchor, he shared a workspace with me. Tom became like another son as he turned to me for professional and personal advice. I assisted him in preparations for contract negotiations and dating apps! The maternal side of me even urged him to let to track his location on the Find My Friends app, so I could keep tabs of his whereabouts when he went on blind dates! Just as the relationship between parent and adult child evolves, Tom has transitioned from a young co-worker to part of my friend group. He and his friends add great energy to my group of middle-aged housewives who meet up for an occasional happy hour or book club!

Though not on nearly as public of a scale, I also experienced this relationship evolution with an incredible young woman named Danielle. She first reached out to me for guidance with a career choice as she graduated from high school, then as she was going through college the first time, and eventually returning to earn a master's degree. Through the years, I have been able to watch as she developed an incredible career, now a vital part of a major foundation team in our community, and has become a mentor herself. Just like the relationship we have with our adult children, there has been a bit of a shift in the dynamic of my relationship with Danielle. As I started writing, no longer was she that young girl who would seek my advice. Since her work at the foundation included proof-reading and editing, I turned my manuscript over to her for her feedback and opinion.

In many ways, the relationships we form with younger people we meet at work or in the community are similar to those we have with our adult children. As a mentor, I was happy to offer these wonderful young professionals pieces of advice and occasional insight along the way, but they did all the hard work and heavy lifting. These young individuals are inspirations to me and are paying it forward to the next generation.

How incredible to think of the way these relationships develop!

Mentorship isn't just found in the workplace. Like churches and neighborhoods, many other places are filled with younger people navigating the challenges encountered in the Growing Up and Juggling Act seasons. As you enter the Empty Nest season, your journey has prepared you to be a significant source of knowledge, wisdom, and support. You, too, can be a mentor—even an informal one—and the Empty Nest season is the perfect season to do so.

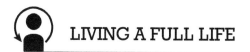 **LIVING A FULL LIFE**

- As you empty the nest, think of a young person you know who you could mentor?
- What do you feel you have to offer a young person seeking your advice or expertise?
- What are the characteristics you would encourage your adult children to find in mentors of their own?

IT CAN'T BE SUNNY ALL THE TIME

Mental pain is less dramatic than physical pain, but it is more common and also more hard to bear. The frequent attempt to conceal mental pain increases the burden: it is easier to say, "My tooth is aching," than to say, "My heart is broken."

C.S. Lewis

Chapter 34
Take The be nice. Pledge

———•———

What mental health needs is more sunlight,
more candor, more unashamed conversation.

Glenn Close

For the past twenty years, I have served on the Mental Health Foundation of West Michigan's board of directors. With the effort to spread more widespread awareness of mental health issues, the organization's mission has expanded significantly during that time. From a push to help chronically mentally ill individuals struggling with addiction and homelessness to a program that goes into schools to help with messages of anti-bullying and suicide prevention.

That push led to the creation of a program called **be nice©**.[27]

It is a simple program concept where the letters of the word "nice" stand for specific words that are part of a curriculum to educate about mental health issues.

- N - Stands for Notice. When we notice what is good and right about a person, we can notice what is different.
- I - Stands for Invite. When we see something out of the ordinary, we need to invite ourselves to have a conversation with the individual displaying behaviors and actions not what we would expect to see.
- C - Stands for Challenge. To challenge stereotypes and excuses someone might use to deflect or give a reason for those behaviors.
- E - Stands for Empowering ourselves to take action. To not just sit by in fear, self-doubt, or insecurity when we see someone who needs our help.

This is just a basic overview of an in-depth and informative program that encourages us to visit the organization's website[28] and spend a few minutes taking the **be nice.** Pledge[29]. The information you discover will equip you with an essential mental health overview that can help you or someone you know.

We know it is important that we treat people well because how we treat people affects how they think, act, and feel; that especially includes how we treat *ourselves*. As empty-nesters, we should pay attention to changes in our feelings, moods, and behaviors, as well as those around us. We can be at a greater risk for developing mental health-related issues during this season. Knowing the warning signs is a vital part of keeping ourselves and the people we love safe and mentally healthy.

 ## LIVING A FULL LIFE

- Are you aware of emotional and behavioral changes in others?
- How about your feelings? What has changed since your children have left the nest?
- What steps could you take in reaching out for help?

Chapter 35
Natural Cycles Menopause And The U Curve

———•———

The curve seems to be imprinted on us as a way to
repurpose us for a changing role in society as we age,
a role that is less about ambition and competition,
and more about connection and compassion.
Jonathan Rauch, *The Happiness Curve: Why Life Gets Better After 50*

The emotional challenges we feel as we enter the Empty Nest season may also correspond with natural emotional cycles tied to reaching this chronological time in our life. We've all heard of the midlife crisis. We see and listen to jokes of a man reaching a certain age (about fifty) and trying to recapture the glory days of his youth by getting a hot young girlfriend and perhaps a sports car. For women, it can be getting a facelift or Botox to combat anxiety about signs of aging and fading beauty, like wrinkles. To top it all off, this time in our life is happening when we are emptying the nest and, for women, going through menopause, thus creating a perfect storm for emotional distress.

Most of us are familiar with menopause, but the research on The Happiness Curve is not as widely familiar. While menopause impacts women (and their partners), The Happiness Curve impacts men and women. Let's begin with The Happiness Curve.

THE HAPPINESS CURVE

Research reveals a U-shaped curve that plots feelings of life satisfaction as we go through the decades of life. The front part of the curve begins at a high point when we are in our teens into our early twenties, the Growing Up season. Then, there is a steady downturn with each passing year where life satisfaction drops. That downward trend coincides with the Young Adult and Juggling Act seasons; our late twenties, thirties, and forties. The bottom of that curve corresponding with turning fifty, just as many of us are likely entering the Empty Nest season.

UPWARD TREND

Then something amazing happens! As our fifties continue, we see a movement upward in satisfaction. As the year-by-year data is plotted, there is a corresponding increase in happiness, satisfaction, and joy in life. This upward trend continues into our late fifties, sixties, and seventies. The data suggests we are as happy in our sixties and seventies as we were in our teens and twenties. This data comes from research conducted worldwide, across many societies, and spanning all socioeconomic levels. Research even shows chimpanzees and orangutans have the same shape in the curve.

However, I'm not sure how researchers could determine that gorillas have a midlife malaise.

HAPPINESS RESEARCH

A book that documents this research is titled *The Happiness Curve.* Researcher Jonathan Rauch analyzed data and created claims, pairing the different emotions and satisfaction levels with different life stages.[30] In his book, Rauch claims the downturn in the late twenties and thirties begins as we start our careers and families, struggling with the financial burdens of paying a mortgage, car payments, and saving for college. At this time in our lives, Rauch points out that as we are struggling to get our careers off the ground, we are sleep-deprived and on stress overload. As we head through the downturn continuation, the bottom-most point in this curve occurs for most of us just as we are emptying the nest. By the time we reach this point in the curve, the slow-and-steady downturn of satisfaction has been a decades-long spiral. We may believe those feelings of discontentment, sadness, depression, and anxiety will be a new normal. It's hard to imagine happiness and joy again. Still, the research proves this to be the time we turn the corner toward a happier life.

LOOKING FORWARD TO THE REBOUND

So, why does this happen for us? A big part of it is that we stop so many of the activities that create stress and enjoy a simpler life. This might be because an empty nest means we have fewer people to care for every day, so we feel less responsibility. Or it might be because by this point in our lives, we are established in our careers and no longer feel the anxiety about performing or over performing.

Of course, the emptiness goes along with the feeling we don't have people depending on us, but the flip side of this feeling can be liberating. One other aspect of this stage in life is that it's the time we're getting grandchildren, with the joy that comes from these new lives and relationships.

MIDLIFE AND MENOPAUSE

Experts in women's health point to the Empty Nest season as coinciding with the significant physical and emotional transition of menopause. Dr. Renee Elderkin, MD, is an Attending Physician/Faculty Member at the University of Michigan-Metro Campus and Associate Professor at Michigan State University. She cares for women through every stage of life, from puberty to childbearing and finally menopause. Dr. Elderkin says one of the most important relationships, as we age, is one with a physician with whom we can honestly discuss ALL aspects of life. As an active member of the Board of Obstetrics/Gynecology and American College of Obstetrics/Gynecology, Dr. Elderkin has cared for women as they have given birth and then followed them through the double-whammy of becoming empty nesters and going through menopause, which can be a time filled with feelings of grief, unworthiness, and uncertainty about the future.

For women entering this stage in life, the biology of menopause produces dramatic physiological changes that produce significant mood fluctuations. In her book, *I Want to Age Like That! Healthy Aging Through Midlife and Menopause*[31], Dr. Diana Bitner, owner of True Women's Health,[32] provides a thoughtful guide through the challenges of the physical transition into midlife. Dr. Bitner, a Certified Menopause Practitioner for the North American Menopause Society, has developed specified treatment programs for women going through menopause. As Dr. Bitner discusses, most women will face challenges around their waistline and in the bedroom as they go through this transitional period in life, including mood changes, hot flashes, decreased sex drive, and night sweats. As with the other aspects of moving from the Juggling Act season into the Empty Nest season, Dr. Bitner and Dr. Elderkin point to this stage as a normal and temporary transition, which most women can navigate with the right information, counsel, mindset, and assistance. If you are struggling, there is help available. You don't need to suffer or make a go of it alone.

HOPE FOR THE FUTURE

For people going through the transition into the Empty Nest season and still feeling on the downward emotional spiral, hang in there! Research shows the upward march on the happiness curve is just around the corner.

 ## LIVING A FULL LIFE

- If you think of your emotions in terms of a spiral, how would you describe the direction that spiral is heading? What changes are you making that are steps to the upward side of the U curve?
- If you are a woman facing physical and emotional challenges related to menopause, have you reached out to your doctor or a menopause expert for help in navigating this series of natural changes in your body?
- If you have reached age fifty, are you feeling like you are on an upward emotional movement?

Chapter 36
Feeling The Grief

———•———

The song is ended—but the melody lingers on.
Irving Berlin

When the Coronavirus Pandemic hit in the spring of 2020, most people went through a tough time because of the loss of so many experiences. There was a lot written about the feelings people were having, which amounted to grief. People felt a sense of loss for what their life used to be and sadness over those experiences they would no longer get to have. Many mental health experts did a deep dive into the different stages of grief, which is similar to what happens when we empty our nest. We are in mourning for the life we used to have. In so many ways, all we want to do is turn back the clock to when life was normal.

That is not how life works.

In fact, it is not surprising to consider how transitioning into an empty nest follows the five stages of grief[33], especially since raising each child from pregnancy to high school graduation spans nearly two decades.

DENIAL

Denial is the first stage because we can't believe something has happened. It might be hard to come to grips with the fact that life, as we knew it for so many years, is over. Life has changed as the last child has moved out, and as with any loss, there is a tendency to believe it can't possibly be the case. Many times, especially in the beginning stages, you may find yourself waiting for that child to walk in the door after school or even absentmindedly set a table place for them at dinner.

ANGER

For some people, this is the next stage. We may be angry at ourselves for not taking advantage of all those moments when our kids were home and we did not fully engage or appreciate them. In this stage, we may be angry at ourselves for those missed opportunities.

BARGAINING

In this stage, we are trying to find a meaning or telling our story. This is a pivotal point, as this marks the time when we move forward into the new reality. This can mean reaching out to others, who may also be entering this stage in life. Telling your story and helping others, is an excellent way to find a purpose.

DEPRESSION

This stage often presents as pain or melancholy. We need to be careful not to allow these overwhelming feelings to take too much control of our lives. During this time, a prolonged period of detachment can signal the need for some professional help. If you find the is the case for you, please reach out for help. This is a normal part of the human experience. If you decide to get help, you will likely find it is only a temporary part of your journey.

ACCEPTANCE

Acceptance is the beginning of an exciting new place in life. Memories of the past are still vivid, but they bring more joy than pain at this part of the cycle. There are moments when you think about the past but are excited for what the future may hold for you. You are happy and fulfilled to think about your children, their years at home, and their new adult lives.

We often think of grief only in terms of death, grief comes during many experiences in our life's journey. For some people, it is the loss of a job or the ending of a marriage. The graduation from school can bring feelings of grief because you know that part of your life is over. Anytime there is an end of any sort, grief can be experienced. Understanding grief and that certain stages are temporary gives us hope for a brighter future as empty nesters.

 ## LIVING A FULL LIFE

- Do you consider the empty nest feelings within the five stages of grief?
- Can you identify feelings you have that fit within these five stages?
- Can you determine which part of the cycle you are in now and take active steps to move into the next stage(s)?

Chapter 31
An Empty Nest Carol

———•———

"I wear the chain I forged in life," replied the Ghost. "I made it link by link, and yard by yard; I girded it on of my own free-will, and of my own free-will I wore it. Is its pattern strange to you?".
. . "Or would you know," pursued the Ghost, "the weight and length of the strong coil you bear yourself? It was full as heavy and as long as this, seven Christmas Eves ago. You have laboured on it since. It is a ponderous chain."
Charles Dickens, *A Christmas Carol*

I'm a huge fan of the Charles Dickens classic *A Christmas Carol*. There have been many modern remixes of this story, using a modified plotline and modern-day references and actors, but the overall story remains.

NEW TAKE ON A CHRISTMAS CAROL

Ebenezer Scrooge is a very wealthy man but a miser. His former partner, Jacob Marley, has passed away and comes back to visit Scrooge as a ghost, along with the spirits of Christmas past, Christmas present, and Christmas yet to come, taking Scrooge on a series of adventures. The Spirit of Christmas Past takes Scrooge back in time. The Spirit of Christmas Present takes Scrooge through the present-day celebrations he is missing. Finally, the Spirit of Christmas Yet to Come takes Scrooge to the lonely ending of his life, should he continue to live as he has been.

One of the central characters affected by Scrooge's miserly life is the child, Tiny Tim, who is disabled and lives in a poor family. Tiny Tim's health and the entire family would benefit if Scrooge were to be more generous.

YOUR VERSION OF THE STORY

Imagine your version of this classic story. Try to imagine ghostly visits to your past, present, and future. Who is your Jacob Marley? Who is your Tiny Tim?

I have imagined my trip through this story, where I travel through my past, present, and future; from life after high school, into the present day, and then into the yet to come. My parents, especially my mom, represent the character Tiny Tim. A Spirit of the Past would take me to my life right after high school, when I was launching out of my parents' nest and into adulthood. A visit to that time in my life makes my heart break over the fact I left without staying in close connection. As I enter the Empty Nest season, I'm overwhelmed with guilt in discovering how much my parents must have missed me and worried about me. This transition must have been even more difficult since there were no cell phones or social media, no texting, FaceTime, Facebook, Snapchat, or other apps.

CLARITY ABOUT THE PRESENT

This time travel exercise may give you perspective and clarity about what's happening now with your children. As I remember leaving my parent's nest, it was only through ignorance of their feelings and emotions that I was not in closer touch with them. I was not looking to escape my parents as much as I was branching out to make my way in the world. The distance, physical and other, was not because I was pushing away from them; I was moving toward my way in life.

As I transition into a fully empty nest, a walk down memory lane with my own Jacob Marley and spirit visitors allows a more complete understanding of the separation. This has been helpful as my youngest graduated from college and started forging her path in life. Even though we have plenty of space at home, I supported her need for freedom and independence as she transitioned from college student to adult. It's so much easier as a parent to adjust to this reality when we fully can't embrace the idea our child is not moving away from us; our child is moving toward making his or her own life.

The Empty Nest season has also spurred me to circle back with my parents, and to schedule more time for activities with them. Life has come full circle. I'm now a frequent visitor to my original nest, just as I hope my birds will eventually find time for frequent trips back home.

LIVING A FULL LIFE

- What do you remember about leaving home?
- What was your relationship with your parents like when you left home?
- How has your relationship with your parents changed as you have emptied the nest?

Chapter 38
Guilt And Grace

———•———

*The beauty of life is, while we cannot undo what is done, we can
see it, understand it, learn from it and change so that every new
moment is spent not in regret, guilt, fear or anger but in wisdom,
understanding and love.*

Jennifer Edwards

Guilt can be another one of those powerhouse emotions that
becomes unbearable during the transitional time into the empty
nest. We look back at those opportunities we didn't take or the
circumstances when we could have done things differently. In the
last chapter, I asked you to take a trip down memory lane, but
sometimes reliving the guilt can become crippling. We think of
those moments when we chose something over our children—an
outing with a friend or a work commitment—and we are filled
with so much regret it can be paralyzing. When it seemed like it
was an endless parade of activities and chores, we never had time

to do anything for ourselves, it seemed like it was an acceptable choice to make. After all, during the crazy years of raising children, so much time, especially free time, is dedicated to kids. So, taking an afternoon or evening and spending it doing something away from the family seemed like a good option. But during the Empty Nest season, it is painful to wish for a commitment with a child and know that when we had those opportunities, we occasionally opted to do something else.

That is where an overwhelming feeling of guilt can settle in.

- We feel guilty for taking time away.
- We feel guilty we did something other than the option that was right ahead of us.
- We feel guilty we squandered the opportunity to fill a few hours of our day with a special activity for our child or children.
- We feel guilty for not appreciating the energy and chaos of the full house.

Hindsight is not 2020. Reality shades the memories we have of looking at those opportunities we wish we had in front of us today.

Unlike a casual game of golf, you do not get to take a Mulligan or a redo. You can't go back in time and make a different decision. Even if you could go back in time, there are just as many chances you would make the same decision all over again. When day after day after day stretches into week after week after week, month after month after month, and year after year after year, it is imperative we make decisions that involve doing something for ourselves. For me, that rarely happened. I can think of only a few opportunities along the way where I missed out on doing something specific with one of my children. My husband and I took a few short getaways with friends or just the two of us, but otherwise, nearly every vacation day, personal day, or comp day was scheduled to be available for one of my kid's activities.

I never wanted to miss anything. Being there and available was a priority for me, and I could not stand the thought of not being there myself to watch, cheer, and experience all those moments for my kids. Perhaps you were this way, too.

It's important when we look back and feel such guilt about missing one or two events along the way, that we remember the next important G-word:

In the Bible, grace is a way to describe being pardoned for something even when we were guilty of doing it. Author Anne Lamott wrote about grace, "I do not at all understand the mystery of grace–only that it meets us where we are but does not leave us where it found us."[34] In our personal lives, and looking back at the growing-up years, we need to give ourselves grace. Hindsight, they say, is perfect, but not when it comes to grace. We tend to beat ourselves up more in hindsight, and guilt becomes a much more overwhelming and much easier feeling to give into. But moving forward meaningfully with the next chapter, stage and season of your life will require giving yourself grace. As the Bible teaches us God extends grace to sinners, likewise, you can extend grace to yourself for parenting decisions that have come and gone.

 ## LIVING A FULL LIFE

- Take out a sheet of paper, think back to those moments that stand out in your life as a parent, and write those moments of guilt that most stand out.

- Try to imagine the circumstances happening at the time you made the decision that causes you guilt.
- Practice forgiveness through those experiences. Give yourself grace.

FLYING LESSONS

———

Autumn leaves don't fall, they fly. They take their time and wander on this their only chance to soar.
Delia Owens, *Where the Crawdads Sing*

Chapter 39
Relationships With Adult Children

———•———

With grown children, we can look back at both our mistakes and what we did well with our parenting, having conversations with a greater degree of honesty than was possible before. In getting older themselves, our adult children may begin to comprehend the burdens and strengths we carried from our own.

Wendy Lustbader

It's challenging for a parent to navigate new relationship dynamics with adult children and welcome new family members as adult children get married and have children. With this transition, many of us get to wear new titles in this stage of the empty nest; mother-in-law and grandmother. With these new titles, we need to adjust to new rules and responsibilities.

As our adult children forge their paths in the twenty-first century, they may move away to pursue educational or professional opportunities. While we celebrate the transition they are making from the Growing Up to the Young Adult season and admire their sense of adventure and ambition, physical distance can make it complicated and challenging to develop the deep relationships we would like to have with them as adults.

We miss seeing them every day but are proud we have raised them to follow their dreams and find their way to make a mark in the world. We may envy watching the adult children of our friends settle nearby in the same city or state, while our kids follow a destiny that takes them to a new part of the country or even the other side of the globe. We yearn to keep our families together, but physical distance creates difficulty as adult children move to new communities or even new states for education or career opportunities. Indeed, physical distance can lead to or even intensify an emotional separation.

EVOLVING RELATIONSHIPS

Whether your adult children live nearby or far away, perhaps the most delicate of all relationships as we empty the nest are the relationships we have with them. Sometimes transitioning is entirely smooth sailing, where the adult child leaves the nest and forms their own life, developing a new type of relationship with their parents. This new adult-to-adult relationship may seem like adult children are developing a friendship with their parents. Perhaps your adult child will invite you to join in special outings with their friends or become your partner in a bowling or golf league. This is a special and magical evolution, marking the parent and child's continued connectedness while entering into a fun new stage that can sometimes be celebrated as a peer-to-peer relationship.

However, in other cases, an adult child will look back on their growing-up years and feel as though those weren't the glory days.

Growing up was tough. The stress of academics, extracurricular activities, friendships, peer pressure, and societal pressure might make some children look back at the Growing-Up season through less than rose-colored glasses.

Raising a child involves setting rules, establishing boundaries, providing structure and discipline in the hopes the child becomes a young adult who is self-reliant and self-sufficient. It's almost ironic to think the better job we did during the Growing-Up season as parents will translate into a more independent grown adult who will seem to need us even less. Perhaps you feel this way, too. We want to be needed by our adult children but feel conflicted or hurt by their need for independence.

The balance is never easy to achieve, resulting in some children looking back at their childhood as an easy time, while others will look at the rules, structure, and discipline as harsh, unyielding, and unfair. As parents now try to create adult relationships with those adult children, a tug-of-war can sometimes ensue.

LOOKING BACK AT THE PAST

We all have our memories and versions of reality. An adult child may look back on their growing-up years and remember certain occasions where things didn't exactly go their way. A strong-willed child may remember those episodes as battles for control of a situation or relationship.

Sorting all this out can be challenging and sometimes painful. Trying to achieve new relationships with grown children can represent hurt feelings brought on by difficult, conflicted, or even buried memories of the Growing-Up season. As parents, we must be willing to admit we may not have had all the answers, and occasionally we may have done or said things our child found offensive or hurtful. That doesn't mean only saying "I'm sorry" or trying to convince your child they are wrong or not entitled to their feelings. Your adult child may find comfort if you take the time to listen and try to understand their painful memories.. If you are interested in mending or moving the relationship forward, you will need to be sincere and authentic in your approach to these difficult conversations.

WALKING ON EGGSHELLS

In her book, *Walking on Eggshells*, Jane Isay traveled all over the country and interviewed dozens of parents and dozens of grown children, nearly seventy-five people in all.[35] Isay shares the tug-of-war stories of many relationships, where the adult child struggles to assert independence while the parents try to release the grip of control over the child. In her research, Isay discovered most adult children deeply love their parents but want us to respect them as adults.

"I was surprised to find that many people in their twenties and thirties were eager to tell me how much they worry about their relationship with their parents and how much time they spend puzzling how to stay close and still be independent."[36]

Isay reported the process of separation to be challenging but offers the optimistic advice that "since adulthood lasts for decades, we have plenty of time to adjust and get it right."[37]

FAMILY COUNSELING

Sometimes, family dynamics don't improve with time. As adult children leave home and start their own families, the parent-child relationship does not evolve. If this is the case for you and your family, please consider seeking the help of a trained family counselor. A professional counselor provides an independent and unbiased view of difficult situations.

Just a caution: family counselors don't come equipped with magic wands. Working through challenging family issues will be difficult. The right counselor gives perspective and understanding, and with enough time and honesty, can help navigate painful family relationships. Even if the relationship with your adult children doesn't improve as quickly as you would hope, a licensed counselor may help you become stronger emotionally and help improve your mental wellness.

 LIVING A FULL LIFE

- How have you navigated the transitional period from child to adult with your children?
- What have been the most challenging aspects of this transition?
- Where can you turn to find resources of information or support?

Chapter 40
Ready For Takeoff
When Your Birds Are
Leaving The Nest

—●—

To raise a child, who is comfortable enough to leave you,
means you've done your job. They are not ours to keep,
but to teach how to soar on their own.

Author Unknown

Becoming a member of the Empty Nest season means watching your own birds fly away. Watching our adult children take flight and leave the nest is a much easier process when we feel our children are ready to be successful as independent adults. I had some help with this due to a special gift given to me early in my motherhood journey by one of my long-term mentors, Diane Kniowski, a woman who was also my boss for twenty years. She was a working mom and understood the challenges I was facing raising kids while working in a demanding career.

She gave me a book that transformed how I thought of my role as a parent of busy children.

THE GIFT OF SELF-RELIANCE

The book, *Raising Self-Reliant Children in a Self-Indulgent World*, written by H. Stephen Glenn and Jane Nelsen, created inspiring and workable ideas for developing a trusting relationship with children and the skills to implement the discipline necessary to help a child become a responsible adult.[38] There is often a battle between the parenting strategies of leniency versus strictness. This book goes beyond these issues to teach children to be responsible and self-reliant, not through outer-directed concerns such as fear and intimidation, but through inner-directed behavior such as feeling accountable for their commitments.

You may have heard the phrase "helicopter parenting" to describe parents' tendency to do everything for their children. Glenn and Nelsen's book took the exact opposite approach, outlining the vital life skills gained by children raised in a home where they were expected to contribute to the workload. Children who were raised on farms, for example, typically developed strong life skills because they had daily chores vitally important to the operation of the farm. If a child was supposed to feed the animals or change the water for the animals before heading to school and that child did not do it, those animals would not have food to eat or water to drink.

The children in this kind of environment learned lessons of responsibility and accountability, but mostly provided intrinsic knowledge that their contributions were significant. They had a vital role, and the family operation depended on it.

It seems almost ironic that now that my kids have grown into the self-reliant adults, I wanted them to be, I feel melancholy for the time when they needed me. Maybe you feel this way too, realizing your grown children don't need to rely on you for everything anymore. But instead of feeling unnecessary, try celebrating. Raising children who can function on their own as adults is the mark of a job well done. After all, isn't that our goal as we do our job as parents?

 ## LIVING A FULLER LIFE

- How much help (and what type) do you need to give to your adult children?
- If you have an adult child living at home, do you have boundaries and expectations?
- Try to imagine the opposite scenario for your adult child? How would your feelings be different if your adult child was not self-reliant?

Chapter 41
Failure To Launch

—●—

It's going to take a stick of dynamite
to get me out of my parents' house.
Matthew McConaughey in *Failure to Launch*

In the 2006 hit movie, *Failure to Launch*, Matthew McConaughey played a thirty-five-year-old single man still living at home with his parents. The parents were desperately trying to get him to move out, but he refused to budge. The movie is a romantic comedy, but for many families, the idea of adult children living at home is not a laughing matter.

This is a stark reality for a significant number of families because of the Coronavirus Pandemic of 2020. As Michael Kolomatsky reported in a June 25, 2020, *New York Times* article, a record thirty-two million American adults were living with their parents or grandparents in April 2020. According to information he quoted from the U.S. Census Bureau, this was nearly a ten percent increase over the prior year.[39]

Author and podcaster Lizzie Post outlines three important conversation areas for parents and adult children living at home.[40]

- TIMELINE - Set a clear timeline (and deadline) for the living arrangement.
- FINANCIAL CONTRIBUTIONS - Does the adult child help pay the bills or extra expenses?
- EXPECTATIONS - Does the adult child help with chores or housekeeping duties? What about guests/curfews/overnight stays? Other behaviors like smoking and drinking?

If your adult child is still inhabiting the nest, it might be time to make some changes. While economic realities sometimes require adult children to move back in with the parents, important boundaries are essential. Although the temptation might be to fall back into the familiar parent-child role and cook, clean, and do laundry for your twenty-something (or thirty-something), it's time for that adult child to gain the life skills necessary to transition into adulthood.

As parents, we walk a fine line between wanting to take care of and protect our children. At the same time, we must prepare them for life after they leave our nest. Being an empty nester may be a challenging season, but it is a season we need to experience. Our adult children need to fly and build their own nests.

LIVING A FULL LIFE

- If you have an adult child living at home, are you secretly happy your nest is not empty?
- How has your relationship changed and evolved? Is it healthy?
- Do you have boundaries, expectations, and a timeline?

Chapter 42
Wedding Bells

●

Keep your mouth shut and wear beige!
Wedding Advice to Mothers of the Groom

The first time I ever heard this phrase was when my son Jacob got engaged. He was marrying his high school girlfriend Taylor, who we had known for several years and already seemed like a part of the family. While she would have never told me to "keep my mouth shut," when it's time for one of your children to get married, the truth of the situation is simple: it's not about you. Your biggest job is to keep your opinions to yourself and not do or wear anything that will draw attention from the bride-to-be.

Planning parties and gatherings are not my forte. I don't have that designing gene. I know what I like when I see it but figuring out how to make an event come together or coordinate something is not my strong suit. So, even if tradition dictated the groom's mother was in charge of everything, I still would not have felt comfortable taking the lead. That said, Taylor is such a warm and welcoming person I couldn't imagine her not welcoming my thoughts and ideas.

I think the above quote is hilarious. It applies not only to the wedding, though. I've learned an umbrella statement that illustrates an essential concept for empty nesters: you are no longer the primary person in control of your child's life. Nor should you be. As a college graduate in his twenties, my son was ready to be a grown-up, launching into the world. He was also ready to become a husband.

MOTHER OF THE BRIDE

The saying applies to mothers of brides, too. Almost exactly a year after Jacob was married, my daughter Jacqueline married her high school sweetheart, Ben. As with Jake and Taylor's wedding, it was best and appropriate to let the bride and groom take control of the planning and decision-making. Fortunately, Jacqueline and Taylor are two of the most organized young women I know, so I developed peace as I kept a "hands-off, mouth closed" approach in letting both brides take charge in planning these significant events.

CELEBRATING A NEW BEGINNING

A wedding is a celebration of the beginning of a new family. It marks the true emancipation of the adult child from the family of his or her childhood. Watching our adult children plan their wedding day is like the time we ran alongside their bicycles, helping them balance without the training wheels or sitting in the passenger seat as they were learning to navigate the roadways as student drivers. In both cases, we were helping them adjust to a period of separation from us and move toward newfound independence.

Observing the wedding day planning is quite similar, though planning for this final transition gives the mother of the bride or groom the chance to adjust to this new role in our child's life. Instead of feeling left out of the decision-making, we can view this period as one where we are free to take care of ourselves. Here, we go from being center stage to a member of the audience. If we play our cards right, we just might get to sit in the front row to watch the show!

One (actually two) additional blessings I have received with my children's marriages have been the opportunity to become connected to two more families of faith. The two mothers-in-law of my adult children have become important women in my life. We share a unique, common bond as praying mothers over the same family we helped create. In my life, Judy (the mother of my daughter-in-law, Taylor) and Ellen (the mother of my son-in-law Ben) are women I count as sisters, knowing these are two women who gave birth to and raised the woman and man my son and daughter fell in love with and have taken for their life partners. I feel blessed by these incredible women who have a special place in my life and heart. Since my married children married "youngests" in their families, those nests also became empty with the marriages.

 ## LIVING A FULL LIFE

- Were you able to take a backseat in the planning of your child's wedding?
- What is your relationship with your child's mother-in-law? (Explore the potential new friendship that could result from this special bond.)

- Are there other significant occasions in your adult child's life where you should stop yourself from offering your opinions?

Chapter 43
Nanaville
The Best Part

—●—

There are really only two commandments of Nanaville:
love the grandchildren and hold your tongue.
Anna Quindlen, *Nanaville*

Nothing could have ever prepared me for the emotion I felt when I became a grandmother. When we hold our child for the first time, the emotion we get is an incredible feeling, but to hold in your arms the child of your child is more precious than words could ever express.

The emotions flood in and you are overcome with love. Love for this new life; and a more profound love, respect, and admiration for your child who has brought this new life into the world. There is also the feeling of hope in the unimaginable future of new life. There is a feeling of mortality in knowing this child will have decades beyond those you exist. There is a feeling of nostalgia in knowing the time has flown from the time the doctor placed your child in your arms in a moment very similar to this one.

A NEW ROLE

At the precise moment of their birth, you know you would lie down your life for this child; and for your child who brought this life into the world. But, at that precise moment, you may also realize these emotions you're feeling take a backseat. You are not the pilot or copilot in this little one's life journey. You have a new role to fill, and like everything else about life with an adult child, this is a delicate balance to figure out what your role will be in the life of this grandchild.

I am new to this part of the journey, so I don't have it all figured out yet. What I have tried to do during this part of the journey is to enjoy every precious moment I get with my sweet grandchild and let his parents know I am available for anything they need at any moment. I even dropped everything and drove to the airport in a snowstorm with a two-hour notice to hop on a plane to fly to Florida when my little grandson was sick. Due to work and higher education commitments, my daughter and her husband needed some help. I was blessed to have the flexibility to allow this grandma to come to the rescue!

Yes, I would do anything for this life.

A big part of the transition into life in Nanaville includes keeping healthy boundaries. Boundaries become so important. You will want to make sure you are offering to help, but not be pushy. Your role is to be supportive but not overbearing. Loving, but not possessive. You need to learn that respecting your child's household rules is one of the truest ways a grandparent shows love. A supportive grandparent does not undermine the authority of the parents. You will help reinforce a critical life lesson to your grandchild about respecting authority. Lead by example and show you respect the rules established by your adult children even when it comes to bedtime and candy!

Enjoy the flood of love this new life brings into your life. Enjoy it and strengthen it by respecting the boundaries of your adult children. You will make a wonderful grandma.

 ## LIVING A FULL LIFE

- Who are your role models for being a grandparent?
- Did you ask your child for a definition of what is expected during this newly forming set of relationships? If not, consider asking. Ask them about their hopes, needs, and expectations.
- Close your eyes and imagine five years from now, ten years, fifteen years, twenty years, and so on. What do you envision your role in the life of your grandchild?

BLESS THIS NEST

———

DEEPEN (OR DISCOVER) YOUR FAITH

As for me and my house, we will serve the Lord.
Joshua 24:15

Chapter 44
Discovering Faith

—•—

For this is what the Lord has commanded us:
"I have made you a light for the Gentiles,
that you may bring salvation to the ends of the earth."
Acts 13:47

My journey of faith began in my twenties. During my Growing Up years, our family would occasionally go to church for one of the big holidays, perhaps Christmas Eve for the candlelight service, or dress up with a new hat and dress for a service on an occasional Easter Sunday, but we were not actively involved in the church.

As a result, I grew up not knowing much about faith. I did not understand the difference in the holidays. I knew Christmas was a holiday where the celebration was to honor the birth of Christ (because of the nativity), but I didn't truly realize the significance and importance of the hope that comes from the resurrection of Jesus Christ celebrated on Easter Sunday. I also did not have something that became the cornerstone of my adult life: a relationship with Jesus Christ.

A GOOD HOME

Let me be clear; I grew up in a good home. My parents were hard-working people who loved my brother and me and did everything they could to provide for us. We had enough food to eat, a warm and dry home with clean clothes to wear. We were never mistreated or abused. My parents also prioritized education and paid for us to earn a college education.

But I did not realize I was missing something so important. For so many years, I missed out on developing the most important relationship I would have in my life.

DISCOVERING FAITH "ON THE JOB"

Early in my career as a television news reporter, I received an invitation (from a virtual stranger) that would lead me into a personal relationship with Jesus Christ.

As I wrote in an earlier chapter, I became a television news reporter right out of college. I had studied everything I thought I would need to know to become a great reporter. I learned how to do interviews, write news stories, do research, even shoot and edit the videotape. As I entered the world of broadcast news, I felt prepared to tackle every aspect of my industry's new role.

Unbeknownst to me, I was missing something significant. I was not prepared for the *humanity* that was at the central part of my new career. I did not take a class that would prepare me for how I was going to *feel*, as a human being, when I reported some of the most tragic occurrences in life. There was no part of the curriculum that prepared my classmates and me for our emotional experiences on the front lines.

The day in the life of a television news reporter frequently involves going to the scene of breaking news: a shooting, murder, stabbing, car or plane crash, drowning, or house fire. It was my job to go to the scene of these terrible events that were happening or had just happened and gather information to report to our viewers. I became an observer and witness to some of the most terrible occasions happening to people. Not only did I witness the grief, despair, and pain of these people, I had nothing in my college background that prepared me for how I was going to feel when I was covering these tragic events.

Day by day, and week by week, as my career unfolded, I became more confident on the outside, but significant changes were happening to me on the inside. I went from someone outgoing and happy to someone who was increasingly nervous and withdrawn. I had a hard time understanding why so many bad things happened. I had an even more difficult time comprehending how people could ever put their lives back together again after a tragic event.

As the months went by, negative emotions took over my life. I compartmentalized my existence; confident and competent at work, but nervous and isolated while I was off duty.

A DIVINE ASSIGNMENT

After an emotional week of covering one of the most tragic events of my entire reporting career to that date, I was surprised by a low-key and heartwarming story assignment I received on a Saturday morning.

Twice a year, many churches in the community where I worked would get together to have an event called a Hunger Walk. Volunteers spearheaded it from several bodies of faith who would raise money and collect a tremendous amount of canned and non-perishable food items. The mission was to restock the shelves at the local food pantry. During the fall season, it was a pretty simple task to inspire people to be generous with their donations, as it was a time heading into the colder winter months and holiday season.

But summer was always a challenging time for the food pantry. With schools out of session, children who could typically get a couple of meals each day at school needed to get all their food requirements met by their own families. For families that already had a limited food budget, summer vacations were often budget-breakers.

Due to this increased need and the expected decrease in donations, the event organizers asked local television news stations to give additional coverage to their cause. I was the reporter assigned to cover this story.

The interview subject that day was a woman who was the main organizer of this event. As I asked her questions for information for the story, she started naming off the churches represented at the event that day. In the middle of rattling off the list, she abruptly stopped and asked me, "Where do you go to church?"

I was a little surprised at the question, as interview subjects rarely asked questions back to the reporters.

I said, "Me? I don't go to church."

She looked at me with a very puzzled look on her face, so I felt obligated to follow up with, "I've never really gone to church, plus I am very busy and work most weekends at the television station, anyway."

FAITHFUL INVITATION

She politely interrupted my litany of excuses and explained she asked the question because she wondered whether I attended one of the churches taking part in that day's efforts. She continued by saying, "Well, if you don't have a church, I would like to invite you to come to my church."

She told me the name of the church and wrote the church's address on a piece of paper.

"Our service starts at 9 a.m.," she said. "I would truly love to see you sometime soon."

With that, we said goodbye and I headed back to the station to put together my report for the six o'clock news.

My next divine encounter with this special lady would happen much sooner than I expected, as I was assigned a story for the late evening newscast the next day. This meant I would not need to arrive at the station to begin my workday until early Sunday afternoon. Because of this flexibility in my schedule, I decided I would go to her church the next morning, so I would not disappoint her.

A MORNING OF SURPRISES

That Sunday morning was filled with surprises. I surprised myself by finding my way to the church. Even though I am a meteorologist, I am directionally challenged and get lost easily. This was years before cell phones and digital maps.

I was also surprised by the beautiful sound of the bells ringing in the church steeple. It was a soothing and welcoming sound, which I had missed out on because I was either fast asleep or at work on a typical Sunday morning.

EPIPHANY

As I walked into the church's interior and made my way toward the sanctuary, I was handed a church bulletin.

Stepping inside the sanctuary, I stopped and looked up at the cross hanging above the pulpit on the back wall and felt the most incredible feeling of peace wash over me. A warm feeling surged through my body and especially into my chest. My heart, really. It was an almost magical feeling that told me I *belonged* in this special place.

There are no words to fully describe the feeling, but it is something I will never forget!

I don't remember a lot about that first Sunday church service. I remember looking at the choir as they were singing from the traditional hymn book and thinking they were the happiest-looking people I had ever seen singing in my entire life.

HOW DO I JOIN?

After the church service was over, I went to the fellowship area to find the woman who had invited me there. I wasn't sure I would recognize her, as I had spent little time with her, but she picked me out, came right over, and welcomed me. She seemed surprised I was there, which was interesting because I was only there because I was worried I would disappoint her if I did not show up.

I thanked her for the invitation and explained this was a rare instance of me not having to work on a Sunday morning. I told her I enjoyed the experience so much I wondered if I could "sign up" to come again in the future if I had another Sunday morning off.

She looked at me with a puzzled look and laughed a little. She said to me, "Honey, you don't have to sign up to come here! Our doors are open to you all the time!" She offered me another invitation. "But there is something you can sign up for if you are interested in learning more about the Christian faith and this church in particular. We have membership classes that meet one time a week for about a month."

PROFESSION OF FAITH

I signed up for the membership class and joined with a few other people interested in learning more about the church and the Christian faith. At the end of that series of classes, I stood before the congregation, and as a single, young woman in her twenties, I made my public profession of faith in Jesus Christ.

A verse from the Bible that has become a favorite of mine is John 16:33, "I have told you these things, so that in me you may have peace. In this world, you will have trouble. But take heart! I have overcome the world."[41]

My profession of faith was not the end of that membership class; it was a beginning. It was the very beginning of my Christian journey of faith that continues to this day.

We are not just physical beings; we are spiritual beings as well. Finding peace during the emotional change to life after our children leave home is much easier when we discover, reconnect with, or strengthen our faith.

 **LIVING A FULL LIFE**

- Have you ever considered learning about Jesus?
- Do you remember your first experience with your faith?
- What's holding you back from offering an invitation to someone to visit your church?

Chapter 45
My First In-Depth Bible Study Was *Veggie Tales*

———•———

Therefore everyone who hears these words of mine and puts them into practice is like a wise man who built his house on the rock.
Matthew 7:24

I would compare the development of my faith to the raising of a child. A newborn baby needs to be cared for, nurtured, fed, and corrected. The same is true with the beginning stages in a journey of faith. According to the teachings in God's Holy Word, the Bible, a new believer needs to be encouraged and nurtured so faith questions may be answered in a true and consistent manner.

It can be challenging for a new believer, especially one who is not surrounded by family members or close friends who are also believers. The new believer needs to have a guide in that development of faith. For me, I discovered those guides within the church congregation I joined in Wisconsin, and specifically in relationships with the other members who were in the membership class with me.

Unfortunately, the beginning of my spiritual journey came with the need to change my career, which would allow me to grow and evolve in the television news business. That meant taking a job as a weekend news anchor at a television station in a smaller market, in a different state.

So as my relationship with Jesus Christ was beginning, my relationship with my first congregation of faith was ending. I made two big career moves in only six months, leaving me without a church family to support my new relationship with Jesus Christ.

I eventually took a reporting position at a television station in West Michigan. I honestly assumed I would stay in that market for only a year, but I ended up meeting the man who would become my husband.

Thirty years later, I'm still here. While I couldn't always see how God had been a part of my entire journey, my marriage was no exception. The man I had fallen in love with was a fellow believer. Not only did he have a personal relationship with Jesus Christ, but he had grown up in a home of believers. He had gone through Sunday school, catechism and even attended Christian schools. His faith was firmly rooted from the very beginning of his life.

I embraced my faith because of my deep feelings. My belief in Jesus Christ was because of an epiphany. I could *feel* the Holy Spirit enter my soul. My faith was based on feelings, so I did not know or understand so much of the Bible. I believe the Bible holds the truth for us and God inspired it, but it seemed so difficult to understand in the early stages of my Christian journey of faith.

Enter *VeggieTales*

When my children were young, *VeggieTales*[42] was a new cartoon for kids, but it was so much more than just cute characters and catchy songs.

The main characters, Bob the tomato and Larry the cucumber, told Bible stories through entertaining animated videos children could understand and in a way they could remember.

Each video told Bible stories that paralleled actual stories in the Bible. As I watched videos with my kids, many of the Bible stories came to life for me over and over again. I understood how the Bible fit together and what the stories had to teach us about God.

Of course, *VeggieTales*[43] was only an introduction to some of the most well-known stories in the Bible, but it was a valuable resource for a young Christian to use to help grasp an understanding of God's Holy Word.

The spiritual blessing that comes from the Empty Nest season is the luxury of finding more time for in-depth Bible study. Consider joining a prayer group or attending a Christian women's conference. As with most aspects of the Empty Nest season, this time in our life also offers a tremendous opportunity for us. We can put our physical, emotional, and spiritual needs at the forefront of our life, filling at least some of those hours with the search for peace and hope that comes from a deepening relationship with God.

 LIVING A FULL LIFE

- How did you learn the stories of the Bible?
- Do you study the Bible regularly?
- What can you do to become more familiar with the Bible? Do you know someone you can talk with about the Bible?

Chapter 46
Proverbs 31 Woman

———•———

The Wife of Noble Character

A wife of noble character who can find?
She is worth far more than rubies.

Her husband has full confidence in her
and lacks nothing of value.

She brings him good, not harm, all the days of her life.

She selects wool and flax and works with eager hands.

She is like the merchant ships,
bringing her food from afar.

She gets up while it is still night;
she provides food for her family
and portions for her female servants.

She considers a field and buys it;
out of her earnings she plants a vineyard.

She sets about her work vigorously;
her arms are strong for her tasks.

She sees her trading is profitable, and her lamp
does not go out at night.

In her hand she holds the distaff and
grasps the spindle with her fingers.

She opens her arms to the poor and
extends her hands to the needy.

When it snows, she has no fear for her household;
for all of them are clothed in scarlet.

She makes coverings for her bed;
she is clothed in fine linen and purple.

Her husband is respected at the city gate,
where he takes his seat among the elders of the land.

She makes linen garments and sells them, and supplies
the merchants with sashes.

She is clothed with strength and dignity;
she can laugh at the days to come.

She speaks with wisdom, and
faithful instruction is on her tongue.

She watches over the affairs of her household
and does not eat the bread of idleness.

Her children arise and call her blessed; her husband also,
and he praises her: "Many women do noble things, but
you surpass them all."

Charm is deceptive, and beauty is fleeting;
but a woman who fears the Lord is to be praised.
(Proverbs 31:10–30)

During my early life as a new wife, young mother, and working professional, I often felt overwhelmed in trying to keep it all together. Every day, there seemed so much more to do than there were hours in the day.

THE GUILT OF NOT MEASURING UP

As an empty nester, I still look back on so many areas and think I could have done so much better. I wanted to be a good wife and mother. I wanted my children to have all their needs met. I think of the times I fell short as I attempted to cook, clean, grocery shop, prepare food, keep a clean house, and then go to work and earn a paycheck to help support my family. I also wanted to have time for my husband, but he was often the only person in my life who could take care of himself.

Proverbs 31 is a chapter that describes "a wife of noble character," and it can be overwhelming. Without sufficient time to get everything done, and certainly no time to do it all well, I often fell painfully short of reaching the ideal of the Proverbs 31 woman. It seems like an impossible standard was set in this passage.

In reality, and with a little perspective, I understand that the point of this passage is to let young men know the qualities to look for in a wife and remind men of those things that should be valued in a wife. Instead of viewing this as a checklist of things for women to do and a standard to which women should try to achieve, this passage is intended to be a form of praise and celebration.

PROVERBS 31 FOR EMPTY-NESTERS

Christian writer Van Walton writes about her own painful and emotional journey as her sons grew up and left home.[44] Walton opens her heart to express the loss and grief we feel as our children leave our home, candidly offering words of support and encouragement from her own counseling sessions.

In a section of this blog post called Reflect and Respond, Walton offers these action steps:

- Choose to look forward, not backward. There are truly many more wonderful memories to be made!
- Rejoice in your children's current accomplishments. It's difficult for them to celebrate amidst our grief of letting them go.
- Decide to get involved in a new volunteer opportunity or hobby before the end of the month.

One other aspect of the Proverbs 31 passage is celebrating motherhood's caretaking and nurturing part. The same God who values the things that matter (as we see in Proverbs 31) is the one who will guide you through the emotional Empty Nest season. You can count on Him.

 ## LIVING A FULL LIFE

- What did you find to be the most overwhelming part of being a wife and mother?
- Who did you turn to for inspiration and support during the hard times?
- Do you find peace in reading about other women having the same painful transition into life as an empty nester?

Chapter 41
Find A New Purpose

—•—

It's in Christ that we find out who we are and what we are living for.
Long before we heard of Christ, he had his eye on us,
had designs on us for glorious living, part of the overall purpose
he is working out in everything and everyone.
Ephesians 1:11, *MSG*

What on earth am I here for? This question is likely one the empty nester asks over and over again. After decades devoted to raising children and keeping a household running, the empty nester often wonders about their purpose in life.

Pastor Rick Warren is the author of the *New York Times* Bestseller, *The Purpose Driven Life*. This book is a forty-day spiritual journey to help transform the reader's answer to one of life's central questions, "What on earth am I here for?"[45]

Pastor Warren's guide is a personal, in-depth examination designed to take the reader through a soul-searching journey. The most successful purposes will be aspirational and inspirational, combining our talents, passions, and skills to find something we love to do and are good at doing. Perhaps the process will help the reader figure out how to fit the pieces of life together to find a meaningful way to impact others' lives.

MY PURPOSE AS A PARENT HAS CHANGED

During the years when we are raising our family, it is easy to find we may have multiple purposes, primarily designed to meet the creature needs of our children:

- Food
- Shelter
- Safety
- Education
- Transportation
- Extracurricular activities, like sports, music, theatre, dance, art
- Emotional support and comfort
- Guidance and wisdom
- Structure and discipline

When your children are growing up, you also have the social role of being the most critical person in another human's life. Of course, when our children are infants, they rely on us for everything. That's the case even through the toddler years; during this period, most become a little more self-sufficient; they feed themselves, even though we still need to purchase, prepare, and provide the food; they learn how to go to the bathroom by themselves, and walk, talk, and play. Talking brings a new level of engagement because they can carry on conversations with us. Eventually, they go off to school and year-by-year become more independent at certain things while needing us less and less along the way. During those years, our primary mission will grow and change, but the idea our kids need us gives us a primary sense of purpose. Exhausting and overwhelming with all the tasks we need to do, and most days more to do than time to get it all done every day. The demands during this stage in life give us purpose.

A difficult trap we fall into when our nests are empty is we believe we don't have a purpose.

PRAY FOR A NEW PURPOSE

At this point in our lives, when our kids no longer need us daily, someone else may need what you offer. A call to any church's office will help you find opportunities to help others in your very own community—people who would find help offered by a caring and experienced empty-nester to be a gift from God.

This is how Barb and Gary Baker became an essential part of our family's life during the Juggling Act season. With two young children and two busy careers, I discovered I was pregnant with our youngest child, Jennifer. Already overwhelmed with a busy schedule, I wanted to find a nanny to come into our home to help care for the new baby. Barb was becoming an empty nester but still had no married children or grandchildren. She was looking for a purpose, and we needed her. For much of the Juggling Act season, Barb and her husband Gary became pseudo-family-members. Too young to be considered adopted grandparents, they became a special aunt and uncle. They were critical parts of our lives for a season, the most giving and loving people I could have ever asked God to put into our family for those years.

As Warren says in his book, "God wants to use you to make a difference in his world. He wants to work through you. What matters is not the *duration* of your life, but the *donation* of it." [46]

Opportunities to be used by God may include:

- A few hours of childcare for the overwhelmed single mom.
- Taking a meal to and chatting with a senior neighbor or shut-in.
- Mentoring a child in school through a program like Kids Hope.
- Grocery shopping for a young family or house-bound senior.
- Visiting people in the hospital.
- Making and serving meals following a memorial or funeral service.
- Writing letters to a prisoner.
- Taking in a foreign exchange student.
- Become a foster parent.

INVEST FORTY DAYS IN DISCOVERING YOUR PURPOSE

On Day One, Warren begins by offering a reassuring reminder that we are on this planet because of an almighty creator, God. For the empty-nester, wondering what's left in life now that our time of raising our children is over, Warren states a biblically-based piece of truth.

"It's not about you. The purpose of your life is greater than your own personal fulfillment, your peace of mind, or even your happiness. It's far greater than your family, your career, or even your wildest dreams and ambitions. If you want to know why you were placed on this planet, you must begin with God. You were born **by** His purpose and **for** His purpose."[47]

As I have struggled with transitioning into life as an empty nester, I find my greatest desires are to find:

- A purpose that will fulfill me and help others
- Deeper relationships
- Peace

My journey through *The Purpose Driven Life* has given me a God-centered focus as I find personal answers to the question, "What on earth am I here for?" Consider asking this same question of yourself and turn to God for the answer. His response may be a surprise. He wants to use you to bless others.

Could you be the Barb and Gary Baker for a family struggling through the Juggling Act season?

 ## LIVING A FULL LIFE

- Do you wonder, "What on earth am I here for?"
- Are you searching for a new purpose in the Empty Nest season?
- Would you be willing to invest forty days in a personal journey?

Chapter 48
Be On Guard For The Attack Of The Enemy

———•———

Be alert and of sober mind. Your enemy the devil prowls around like a roaring lion looking for someone to devour.
1 Peter 5:8

Robert Frost's poem, *The Road Not Taken*, begins with these well-known lines:

Two roads diverged into a yellow wood
And sorry I could not travel both

There are many times in my life when I would describe myself as being double-minded, or standing at the divergence of two roads, sorry I couldn't travel both of them. I would decide which road to take and then spend countless hours questioning myself about the wisdom of the decision. Many decisions I would make would lead to my waffling back-and-forth, thinking about and wondering whether I had made the correct decision. This guessing would often lead me to change my mind, maybe even multiple times, going back-and-forth between the different choices I could've made. Not only revisiting those decisions made but wondering how things would be now if I had made other choices. If we aren't careful, we can allow ourselves to question every single decision we've made.

DECISIONS ABOUT THE FUTURE

The Empty Nest season comes complete with many life decisions to make. Unfortunately, in this stage, being double-minded can be almost crippling.

- Do I move forward in my current career, or make a change?
- Do I retire and enjoy leisure time?
- Do I downsize our home or move to a brand-new community?
- Do I stay where I am?
- Do I pursue a new hobby or sport?
- Am I satisfied with my friendships and relationships?

Depending upon whether you are married and what's going on in your spouse's life, these decisions may be even more challenging.

As we have explored in earlier sections of this book, decisions we make in the Empty Nest season can leave us with a feeling of uncertainty, self-doubt, or even confusion. I believe the sinister nature of the one the Bible describes as "the enemy" is hard at work during these times of uncertainty and self-doubt. Any tiny little seed that has been planted will be watered, fertilized, and eventually pruned and shaped by the evil one. Satan would like nothing more than to freeze our progress and keep us churning away in the transitional period, blocking the progress we need to move into a fulfilled stage of the empty nest.

CAUGHT BETWEEN THE BOAT AND THE SHORE

Imagine getting onto a boat to take a trip. If we refuse to make decisions, it's as though we have one foot on a boat ready to leave while the other foot is planted on the shore. The boat is pulling away. We must decide where we are going and not allow ourselves to remain stuck in that transitional phase. If we don't commit to one side or the other, we will fall into the water. However, in life, what we fall into is not simply a body of water; it is a pit of despair and disappointment, sadness, or depression. We are caught between being stuck in reliving our past lives or moving toward the future. The enemy delights in the turmoil this causes for us. If we are not careful, we will put off making decisions, procrastinating the very choices that will help us out of any funk.

We need to realize deciding to move forward is a liberating part of life's journey. Emotional freedom comes from taking steps in a new direction. (Even if they are baby steps.)

By the way, I've discovered the best strategy for keeping the enemy at bay is to turn to God in prayer. When I feel alone, sad, or in despair, prayer provides comfort and hope, especially during the most challenging and difficult times. The lyrics of the wonderful song "What a Friend We Have in Jesus" illustrates God's loving friendship and the power of prayer.

What a friend we have in Jesus
All our sins and griefs to bear
And what a privilege to carry

Everything to God in prayer

Oh, what peace we often forfeit
Oh, what needless pain we bear
All because we do not carry
Everything to God in prayer

Have we trials and temptations?
Is there trouble anywhere?
We should never be discouraged
Take it to the Lord in prayer

Can we find a friend so faithful?
Who will all our sorrows share?
Jesus knows our every weakness
Take it to the Lord in Prayer

LIVING A FULL LIFE

- Are there areas of your life where you feel most undecided?
- Do you feel conflicted when you make a decision or when you have made a decision?
- Do you have a prayer partner who can help you stay strong during these times?

Chapter 49

Have You Heard About MOPS? Shouldn't There Be A GOPS?

———•———

Therefore encourage one another and build each other up,
just as in fact you are doing.
1 Thessalonians 5:11

At most churches, there is a local group part of an international organization called MOPS. MOPS is an acronym for Mothers of Preschoolers. The organization started in the 1970s as a support group (of sorts) for young moms. In many churches, it is a vital epicenter for young women to come together to support and encourage each other through the often-tumultuous journey of mothering young children in the chaotic season of raising a young family. The main groups typically meet every week or every other week during the school year, even arranging on-site childcare so these moms can engage, connect, and socialize with their peers.

This organization has grown significantly through the years, with chapters found in over sixty countries. Indeed, a great lesson is that people are people, and moms are moms, no matter what language they speak or their skin color.

Many of the weekly meetings include Bible story and spiritual development activity, in addition to refreshments. The fellowship is perhaps the most vitally important part of these gatherings, as these women share so much about life with one another, turning to each other for guidance, support, and advice. They share laughter, tears, and vow to consistently pray for one another through times of hardship and trials in life.

THE NEXT STAGE (MOMSnext)

Besides expanding geographically, MOPS has expanded through the years to include a MOMSnext group designed for moms with older kids who still seek to continue these special connections and unique communities. This next group also provides emotional and sometimes physical support many mothers need as children transition to the next stage in life. While there aren't as many of the MOMSnext groups, those that are active provide at least twice-monthly meetings, with more flexibility in schedule, activities, and curriculum.

WHAT ABOUT THE EMPTY-NESTERS? (GRANDPARENTS OF PRESCHOOLERS - GOPS)

I've often thought the MOPS organization should create an extension of their program and call it GOPS (Grandparents of Preschoolers). There is perhaps an even more significant lack of social connectedness and challenging change to make when our homes are no longer filled with the chaos and activity that comes with raising children. This group would be open to anyone adjusting to this new stage in life, when the kids are leaving the nest, getting married, and grandchildren come along. So, even though the blessing of being a grandparent of a preschooler may not have happened yet, anyone adjusting to this new life stage would be welcome in the organization.

There is a need for a special connection and the development of a close relationship with a fellow believer during this challenging adjustment period. Our children are getting married and building their nests. A time when having a special group of fellow believers who are also going through or who have already gone through this same period of change can prove to be the most important and comfortable relationships we can build.

Since this type of organization does not exist (yet), perhaps you could consider pulling together your own group. Invite friends from work, church, or your neighborhood to meet regularly to discuss the issues everyone is facing, has faced already, or will face in the future. Get creative! Structure the meetings like a book club or discussion group—schedule outings and adventures. Encourage the rest of the group to invite people they know in the same life stage. You may find excellent new relationships evolve from a group of fellow believers who can learn to understand, trust and lean on one another to find peace, joy, and hope in this new season of life.

 ## LIVING A FULL LIFE

- Do you have a group of Christian peers to meet with regularly?

- Are there certain life experiences you would love to share with others?
- What are the benefits of meeting regularly with a group of Christian peers?

Chapter 50
Embrace The Quiet Time

———•———

And the peace of God, which transcends all understanding,
will guard your hearts and your minds in Christ Jesus.
Philippians 4:7

Transitioning into the empty nest means the house is often silent. Where there used to be pandemonium, chaos, noise, music, laughing, dancing, yelling, and sometimes fighting, it is now often stillness. While maybe not literally, the quiet can seem deafening.

This quiet time also provides an excellent opportunity to reconnect yourself with God. This is an opportunity for quiet times of prayer and reflection. Psalm 46:10 says, "Be still and know that I am God; I will be exalted among the nations, I will be exalted in the earth."

Our time to nurture our spiritual life is no longer only what we can cram in between other activities and chores. We have the opportunity to sit down and read the Bible, write in a prayer journal, and spend time truly listening for God's voice in our lives.

LISTEN FOR GOD'S VOICE

When our nest was full and our days were overwhelmingly busy, we would have to strain to hear God's voice in the storm. Now, we can hear God's whisper to us in the calm. When we feel there is no one to listen to us and no one to communicate with, we know there is always one essential relationship we have who has a dedicated listening ear when we need it the most.

We are never alone. When our nest may seem big and empty, God is there. Just as he was during the chaotic years, those years when we only cried out for help to get everything we needed to accomplish done. This time around, we need the reassurance that the calm, quiet, and stillness were a part of God's journey for us as well.

DEDICATED PRAYER TIME

Call on me and come and pray to me, and I will listen to you.
Jeremiah 29:12

God says in Jeremiah, "Call on me and come and pray to me, and I will listen to you." (29:12). Yet, our prayer life and spiritual development were probably put on the back burner for so many years. We just could not find enough quiet time in the day. We were exhausted and weary. It is in this season while our nest seems so empty, our spiritual life may indeed become full. Perhaps fuller than ever before for so many of us.

 ## LIVING A FULL LIFE

- How has your prayer life changed since becoming an empty nester?
- How does the quiet make it easier for you to hear God's voice?
- Do you have a specific routine for prayer and devotional time? If not, consider creating one. This is one of the best ways to ensure you will live fully as an empty nester.

Conclusion
Write A Letter To Your Eighty-Something Self

———●———

What if we took Brad Paisley's song, "Letter to Me," and flipped it around? What if, instead of writing an encouraging note to our younger selves, we took some time to write a message to our older selves? What would be put in the letter?

At the beginning of this book, the letter was about looking back at the history of the life we have led to this point. We already know what has happened. Make this letter from your future self more aspirational!

Take a few minutes today and write a short note to yourself, thirty years in the future. Write about your hopes, dreams, and concerns. Write about the things you plan to accomplish and the people you will lean on when times get tough. There's so much life left to live. Live fully during these next thirty years.

Dear Eighty-six-year-old Terri,

As you read this letter, you will find it hard to believe how quickly these three decades have gone by. Right now, life is filled with uncertainty, anxiety, sadness, and a bit of excitement.

The world in your mid-fifties was in a state of uncertainty and generated by a global pandemic, the Coronavirus. So many life plans were being changed and canceled. People were suffering, some from the virus and others from the impact of social distancing and shutdowns the government put into place to stop the virus's spread. Millions of people were unemployed. The country was experiencing civil unrest and, in some cases, riots in cities large and small.

Professionally, you weren't sure what the future would be for a woman entering her late fifties who had spent her entire professional career in front of a television camera. As you saw the wrinkles and aging lines emerge, you wondered how much longer there would be a place for you in the media.

As you looked back at your career, you wondered whether the sacrifices you made to get to this point in your career were appreciated, noticed, or even remembered.

The pride you felt in your family was what you felt was your best accomplishment. Even though you missed them terribly, you realized Jacob and Taylor were forging a wonderful life together! You were proud of Jacqueline, Ben, and baby Levi (he was a toddler and is now in his early thirties). And of course, this was the year your nest became empty as Jennifer headed out to make her own adventures.

Your children (and grandchildren) have grown up to love the Lord and are making a tremendous impact helping to make the world a better place for everyone, especially those in need!

Bill, your true partner in life, has used his incredible leadership skills and understanding of human nature to shape public policy and create solutions for some of the biggest problems facing so many people. You couldn't be prouder of him.

As for you, you have continued to chase your dreams and discovered incredible blessings from God along the way. You have learned to lean on God during the challenging times, as you lost friends and loved ones. Your spiritual journey has allowed you to look for peace in times of uncertainty, hope when you faced disappointments, and companionship when you felt all alone.

I wish I could give you a glimpse into the future, which still has so much for you to accomplish!

Your fall and winter seasons will be your best once you have embraced the idea that seasons must change.

Even though you have a hard time releasing your grip on the past, please know joy and purpose will come when you realize it's a good thing that it "Can't be Summer forever."

I'm so proud of you!

Fifty-six-year-old Terri

About the Author

As a television meteorologist, **Terri DeBoer** has delivered West Michigan's "wake up" weather for three decades. She also co-hosts a daily lifestyle show, eightWest.

Terri's public journey through the seasons in life, from on-air pregnancies to the marriages of two children and becoming a grandmother, gives her a special connection with other moms and grandmothers. She now shares lessons from her most challenging season of life: adjusting to the quieter life in an empty nest.

Terri resides in Byron Center, Michigan. Connect with Terri at www.terrideboer.com.

Notes

1 These definitions come from a combination of Google, dictionary.com and Merriam-Webster.com. I used multiple sources to develop a full definition because the idea of seasons, is so important for us to understand life's changes.

2 *New International Version*

3 Definition by Google Dictionary. https://www.google.com/search?q=google+dictionary&rlz=1C1GCEV_en&oq=google+dictionary&aqs=chrome..69i57j0i433j0j0i433j0l4.3678j0j7&sourceid=chrome&ie=UTF-8#dobs=essential

4 www.mayoclinic.org Article written by Mayo Clinic Staff Dated August 24, 2019

5 Ibid. .

6 https://publishingperspectives.com/2011/05/200-million-americans-want-to-publish-books/

7 https://www.literatureandlatte.com/scrivener

8 https://www.huffpost.com/entry/the-10-health-benefits-of-dogs-and-one-health-risk_n_57dad1b8e4b04a1497b2f5a0

9 https://petsforvets.com/

10 https://www.petsforpatriots.org

11 This is a private group with more than 9,500 members. https://www.facebook.com/groups/emptynestcommunity/

12 www.grownandflown.com

13 Oxford University Press On-line Dictionary

14   https://www.forbes.com/sites/nextavenue/2018/07/01/going-back-to-college-after-50-the-new-normal/#5667504131ff

15   https://www.pewresearch.org/fact-tank/2018/09/24/stay-at-home-moms-and-dads-account-for-about-one-in-five-u-s-parents/

16   https://www.salary.com/articles/stay-at-home-mom/

17   https://www.aarp.org/work/working-after-retirement/info-10-2013/ready-for-your-second-career.html

18   https://encore.org/

19   Workman Publishing Company, 2012

20   https://workforyourself.aarpfoundation.org/

21   https://www.ted.com/talks/mel_robbins_how_to_stop_screwing_yourself_over?language=en

22   www.girlsontherun.org

23   https://www.medicalnewstoday.com/articles/325353

24   www.sleepfoundation.org

25   https://www.investopedia.com/articles/personal-finance/090415/cost-raising-child-america.asp

26   Gladwell, Malcom. *Outliers*, Little, Brown and Company, 2008.

27   https://www.benice.org/

28   https://www.benice.org/

29   https://www.benice.org/take-the-pledge

30   Rauch, Jonathan. *The Happiness Curve*, Thomas Dunne Books, May 2018.

31   https://truewomenshealth.com/product/i-want-to-age-like-that-healthy-aging-through-midlife-and-menopause/

32   https://truewomenshealth.com/

33   The Stages of Grief is attributed to the Kubler-Ross model: Kubler-Ross, E., 1972. "On Death and Dying." *JAMA: The Journal of the American Medical Association*, 221(2), pp.174–179.

34   Lamott, Anne, *Traveling Mercies,* Patheon, 1999.

35   Isay, Jane. *Walking on Eggshells,* Flying Dolphin Press,

March 2007, p. xiii.

36   Ibid p. xiii

37   Ibid p. xv

38   Glenn, H. Stephen and Jane Nelson. *Raising Self-Reliant Children in a Self-Indulgent World*, Harmony, 2000.

39   https://www.nytimes.com/2020/06/25/realestate/more-adults-than-ever-live-with-parents-or-grandparents.html

40   https://www.houzz.com/magazine/the-polite-house-how-to-set-rules-for-adult-children-living-at-home-stsetivw-vs~69012443

41   *New International Version*

42   https://www.veggietales.com/

43   https://www.veggietales.com/dvds-shows/veggietales.html

44   She wrote this article for a wonderful Christian ministry for women called Proverbs 31. https://proverbs31.org/read/devotions/full-post/2012/09/21/emptying-and-filling-my-nest

45   Warren, Rick. *The Purpose-Driven Life*, Zondervan, 2002.

46   Ibid. p. 233

47   Ibid., p.17.

A free ebook edition is available with the purchase of this book.

To claim your free ebook edition:

1. Visit MorganJamesBOGO.com
2. Sign your name CLEARLY in the space
3. Complete the form and submit a photo of the entire copyright page
4. You or your friend can download the ebook to your preferred device

Morgan James
BOGO™

A **FREE** ebook edition is available for you or a friend with the purchase of this print book.

CLEARLY SIGN YOUR NAME ABOVE

Instructions to claim your free ebook edition:
1. Visit MorganJamesBOGO.com
2. Sign your name CLEARLY in the space above
3. Complete the form and submit a photo of this entire page
4. You or your friend can download the ebook to your preferred device

Print & Digital Together Forever.

Snap a photo

Free ebook

Read anywhere